A PRACTICAL GUIDE TO THE MASTERY
OF SWEDISH

# SWEDISH
## Essentials of Grammar

## Åke Viberg
## Kerstin Ballardini
## Sune Stjärnlöf

**PASSPORT BOOKS**
*NTC/Contemporary Publishing Group*

*Titles Available in This Series:*
Essentials of English Grammar
Essentials of Latin Grammar
Essentials of Russian Grammar
Essentials of Swedish Grammar
French Verbs and Essentials of Grammar
German Verbs and Essentials of Grammar
Italian Verbs and Essentials of Grammar
Spanish Verbs and Essentials of Grammar

*Also Available:*
Handbook for Business Writing

Cover design by Nick Panos

This edition first published in 1991 by Passport Books
A division of NTC/Contemporary Publishing Group, Inc.
4255 West Touhy Avenue, Lincolnwood (Chicago), Illinois 60712-1975 U.S.A.
Copyright © 1984 by Åke Viberg and Bökforlaget Natur och Kultur
Printed in the United States of America

ISBN-13: 978-0-8442-8539-9
ISBN-10: 0-8442-8539-0
14 15 VRS/VRS 0 8

# *Preface*

*Essentials of Swedish Grammar* presents the major grammatical concepts of the Swedish language. For ease of use, the book is divided into 17 chapters organized into manageable sections, each covering a distinct point of grammar. The section number is indicated by two digits: the first (followed by a period) specifies the chapter, while the second indicates the order within the chapter. Thus, in Chapter 4, one would find sections 4.1, 4.2, 4.3, and so on.

Grammar rules are presented in a progressive order, showing how the language is gradually built up. To facilitate study, all grammar terms, even the most basic, are fully defined when they are first introduced. From the very beginning, users learn to form complete sentences, which they are encouraged to extend and modify in increasingly varied ways.

As a further aid to the user, some grammar points are treated several times and integrated with other grammatical structures. For example, subject pronouns are dealt with in Chapter 2, object pronouns (including the reflexive *sig*) in Chapter 5, and the possessive pronouns in Chapter 12. Forms presented early on are generally summarized after the entire system of that structure has been covered. For instance, a brief overview of Swedish verb forms occurs as early as Chapter 2. The most important auxiliary verbs are treated in Chapter 6, while a systematic presentation of *all* verb forms occurs in Chapter 9.

Care has been taken so that the most important grammar points are presented as early as possible within a chapter. As a result, users wishing to understand the salient features of a particular grammar structure may concentrate on the initial parts of a given chapter. A detailed index at the end of the book assures easy location of each item.

Examples illustrating grammar concepts were chosen for their authenticity—to represent the structures most frequently encountered in Swedish speech and writing. Thus, in addition to learning the fundamental rules of the language, users will also acquire a familiarity with the style and vocabulary characteristic of modern Swedish.

*Essentials of Swedish Grammar* is a thorough handbook that lends itself to a variety of uses. Because its basic approach is to provide simple, concise explanations, it can be used by students of varying levels, as well as by those who need a convenient reference to consult on confusing points of grammar. This book can be used for study and review, for individual or group work, as part of a refresher course, or for business, travel, or research.

*Essentials of Swedish Grammar* is a unique and effective language tool. Its authors and the publisher are confident that this comprehensive reference will prove indispensable to all those teaching and studying the language of Sweden.

# Contents

# 1  Introduction

## 1.1  What do you need to learn to speak a new language?

There are many different things you have to learn before you can speak a new language. What most people think of first is, of course, all the new words, the *vocabulary (ordförråd)*. A great many Swedish words are very similar to English words. First, there are all the everyday words that English and Swedish have as a common heritage from the old Germanic languages, words like **finger, hand, syster, son, katt,** and **norr,** and many of the numbers, days of the week and so on. Second, there are a large number of modern international words that are more or less identical in Swedish and English: **hotell, bank, television, politik, sport, fotboll, film, radio** and so on. In fact there are so many Swedish and English words that look the same or nearly the same that you can understand some Swedish texts without knowing any Swedish at all. But the pronunciation is usually different, and anyway there are many Swedish words that are not the same in English, so learning vocabulary will take you a long time.

Sometimes you can guess the meaning of a word from its form or its context, but not always. So you will need to get a *dictionary (ordbok)*, so that you can look up new words and check their meaning and pronunciation. It will also be well worth your while to keep a special *vocabulary book (glosbok)* in which you note down new words and their equivalents in English as you come across them.

When you speak, the words you say are made up of *sounds (ljud)*. For example, with the sounds *b e d* you make the word 'bed'. Many of the Swedish sounds are easy to learn because they are the same or almost the same as in English – sounds like *b, d, f, k, l, m, n, p, s, t, v* and a few more. Other sounds, however, such as most of the vowels and a few consonants, are different. Learning the *pronunciation (uttal)* of these new sounds is part of the business of learning Swedish.

Another problem is *spelling (stavning)* and the *alphabet (alfabet)*. You will find the letters of the Swedish alphabet on the inside front cover. Normally a letter corresponds to one sound only, but there are a number of exceptions to this principle. For example, the letters **c** and **z** represent the same sound as the letter **s**, which is the one most frequently used. (In loan words and names **c** sometimes represents the same sound as **k: calypso, Carin, Carlsson,** etc.) Some sounds, for example, do not have their own letter; they are spelt by using a combination of letters, such as **th** in English. The combinations **sj** or **skj** in Swedish represent one sound, a sound fairly similar to the sound represented by **sh** in English. This Swedish sound occurs at the beginning of words like:

**sjal**   shawl               **skjorta**   shirt

Besides practising the pronunciation of the new sound, you will also have to learn what letter combinations are used to represent it when you write.

There are also two very important features of pronunciation in Swedish which are not marked in writing: *length (längd)* and *stress (betoning)*. As they are not indicated in writing, there is a risk that you will neglect them. But they are fundamental to a good Swedish pronunciation, so read particularly carefully 8.3, where you will find these features explained in detail. But to help you now, here is a short explanation of what is meant by length. *Length* refers to the fact that a vowel sound in Swedish can be either short or long. (See the explanation in 8.3.) In the first of the following Swedish words the *i* sound is long, in the second it is short:

sil   sieve                        sill   herring

To help you learn the pronunciation of new words, special marks may be used to tell you when a vowel is short or long. Such marks are used in certain sections of this grammar, but they are never used in normal written Swedish. A long vowel is marked with a dash (_) under the vowel, and a short vowel with a dot (.), thus:

sil                                sill

A distinction is made between short and long vowels in Swedish only when the vowel is stressed. The meaning of the words *stress* and *vowel* is given in the chapter on pronunciation, 8. We suggest that you read 8.1–8.3 as soon as you have read the next few sections on *grammar (grammatik)*.

To speak a new language you need to learn how words are put together to make sentences. That is what is described in *grammar (grammatik)*.

## 1.2   Why do you have to learn grammar?

Imagine a simple situation when you want to say something in Swedish. You are in a small Swedish town you have never visited before and you can't find any of the places you want to go to. Let's imagine that the town has a bank, a post office, a railway station, a hospital and so on. If you can't find the way to the bank, you can ask a passer-by:

Var är banken?                    Where is the bank?

What do you have to know to be able to ask a question like that in Swedish?

You could, of course, learn the whole phrase **Var är banken?**, but if you go about it that way, you will have to learn a fantastically large number of phrases. However, if you compare our first question with the following ones, you will see that they are all alike:

| | |
|---|---|
| Var är posten? | Where is the post office? |
| Var är toaletten? | Where is the toilet? |
| Var är torget? | Where is the market square? |
| Var är skolan? | Where is the school? |

Just as in English, all the questions are made up of a number of words, in English four or five words, in Swedish three. You can translate the questions almost word for word:

| | |
|---|---|
| (Var är banken?) | var=where, är=is, banken=the bank. |

The word **var** 'where' is a *question word* or *q-word (frågeord)*. Other question words are **när** 'when' and **vem** 'who':

| | |
|---|---|
| När är det? | When is that? |
| Vem är Olof Palme? | Who is Olof Palme? |

To be able to construct a question correctly in Swedish, it is not enough just to know the words. You also have to be able to put them in the right order. This is called *word order (ordföljd)*. Word order is very important in Swedish and it is not always the same as in English. In our examples above, however, the word order is the same in both languages.

Not all questions contain the word **är** 'is'. Here are some other possible questions:

| | |
|---|---|
| När somnar Kalle? | When does Kalle fall asleep? |
| När vaknar Kalle? | When does Kalle wake up? |
| Var arbetar Kalle? | Where does Kalle work? |
| Var bor Kalle? | Where does Kalle live? |

The words which replace **är** in the Swedish sentences are all of the same kind. They are called *verbs (verb)*. Most verbs say what someone does or what happens. So we can make a rule about Swedish that says that the question word always comes first, provided there is a question word. Then the verb must always follow, directly. You can see this in a simple word-order diagram:

| Q-WORD | VERB | |
|---|---|---|
| När | somnar | Kalle? |
| *When does Kalle fall asleep?* | | |
| Var | bor | Kalle? |
| *Where does Kalle live?* | | |
| Vem | är | Olof Palme? |
| *Who is Olof Palme?* | | |

Make questions yourself about some other people with the help of the following question words and verbs. (You can think of the names yourself.)

Question words: **var** 'where', **när** 'when', **vem** 'who', **vad** 'what'.

Verbs: **dansar** 'dance', **sjunger** 'sing', **äter** 'eat', **dricker** 'drink', **skriver** 'write', **läser** 'read'.

Here are some of the questions you can make:

| Vad dricker Kalle? | What does Kalle drink (is Kalle drinking)? |
| Var dansar Kalle? | Where does Kalle dance (is Kalle dancing)? |

If you put in other names instead of Kalle, you can, with the help of this simple rule, make many hundreds of questions. That is typical of the most important grammar rules: they tell you how to construct a virtually unlimited number of new utterances of the type that are called, in grammatical terms, *sentences (meningar)* and *clauses (satser)*.

# 1.3   Sentence and clause

When you speak or write, your words are grouped together in sequences of larger units called *sentences (meningar)* and *clauses (satser)*. In writing, a sentence begins with a capital letter and ends with a full stop, a question mark or an exclamation mark:

| Sven sköt en björn. | Sven shot a bear. |
| Vem sköt en björn? | Who shot a bear? |
| Skjut en björn! | Shoot a bear! |

. *punkt (full stop)*
? *frågetecken (question mark)*
! *utropstecken (exclamation mark)*

In straightforward examples like this the sentence is also a clause. In fact, it is the clause that is the smallest natural unit which is composed of words. So a sentence always consists of at least one clause. The fact that there is a difference between clause and sentence is illustrated by the fact that you can put several clauses together to make a sentence with the help of little words like **och** 'and', **men** 'but' and **att** 'that':

*One clause and one sentence*

| Lisa arbetar. | Lisa works. |
| Sven sover. | Sven sleeps. |

*Two clauses and one sentence*

| Lisa arbetar och Sven sover. | Lisa works and Sven sleeps. |
| Lisa säger, att Sven sover. | Lisa says that Sven sleeps. |

The *comma (kommatecken)* is used in Swedish, as in English, in lists, but never before the words **och** 'and', **eller** 'or', etc. (See 7.3 and 7.4 for use of the comma in sub-clauses.)

| Mona, Peter, Eva och Per bor här. | Mona, Peter, Eva and Per live here. |
| Peter får skjuta en björn, en varg eller en älg. | Peter may shoot a bear, a wolf or a moose. |

# 1.4 Word forms. Endings

Grammar not only describes how words can be combined to make clauses and sentences. It also describes how words can have various forms and how this affects their meaning. Take, for example, the word 'work' in English. In the following sentences it appears in different forms:

He **works** here.
We **worked** all day yesterday.
She is **working** hard.

**work**, **worked** and **working** are different forms of the word 'work'. Different *endings (ändelser)* have been added.

|  | *Ending* |
|---|---|
| work+ | s |
| work+ | ed |
| work+ | ing |

Or take the word 'car'. If you want to talk about more than one car you have to add the ending **s**:

one car      two cars

Every ending has a particular meaning. The meaning 'more than one' is called the *plural (plural)*. There are also plural forms in Swedish. The word for 'car' is **bil**. You make the plural of this word by adding the ending **ar**:

en bil      två bilar

# 2  Word classes

In any language there are various kinds of words, each of which follows a different rule in grammar. To describe this system, words are divided into *word classes* or *parts of speech (ordklasser)*. We have already met one important word class, the verb. As you saw in 1.2, it stands in a particular position in question-word questions. Another typical feature of the verb, as with the other word classes, is that it changes its form in a particular way with particular endings.

## 2.1  The verb and its forms

As we have seen, the verb usually describes *what someone does* or *what happens*. In both English and Swedish the verb has different forms according to *when* someone does something or something happens. This is done by means of a change of form called *tense (tempus)*. 'Tempus' is in fact the Latin word for 'time'. This is the most important change of form in the Swedish verb. The verbs in the following pairs of sentences have different tenses:

| | |
|---|---|
| Olle arbeta**r** idag. | Olle is working today. |
| Olle arbeta**de** igår. | Olle worked yesterday. |
| Olle dansa**r** nu. | Olle is dancing now. |
| Olle dansa**de** för en timme sedan. | Olle danced an hour ago. |
| Olle duscha**r** nu. | Olle is having a shower now. |
| Olle duscha**de** imorse. | Olle had a shower this morning. |

In the first sentence in each pair the verb ends in **r**; in the second sentence in each pair it ends in **de**; **r** and **de** are two possible endings of the verb. The ending **r** shows that something is happening *now*. This is a tense called the *present (presens)*. The ending **de** shows that something happened earlier. This tense is called the *past*, or sometimes the *preterite (preteritum)*.

In English both the present and the past tense have two forms: the simple form and the continuous or progressive form. For example:

| | |
|---|---|
| Peter plays the piano. | *Simple present* |
| He is playing the piano now. | *Continuous present* |
| Ann worked hard yesterday. | *Simple past* |
| She was working all day. | *Continuous past* |

Swedish does not have continuous forms of the verb; it only has the one simple form of the present and of the past, which end in **r** and **de** respectively and which are used to translate both the simple and the continuous forms in English.

| | |
|---|---|
| Lisa arbetar nu. | Lisa is working now. |
| Lisa arbetar varje dag. | Lisa works every day. |
| Telefonen ringde klockan 7. | The phone rang at 7 o'clock. |
| Telefonen ringde hela dagen. | The phone was ringing the whole day. |

As you can see, the Swedish present and past are translated in different ways according to the context.

When you are a beginner, you usually meet a verb in the present form, as in the following sentence:

Sten cyklar.            Sten cycles. (Sten is cycling.)

What do you do if you want to make the equivalent of the following sentence?

Sten cycled yesterday.

To make that sentence you need to know what 'yesterday' is in Swedish. It is **igår**. You also need to be able to change the present form of the verb **cyklar** into the past form. You do so with the help of the following simple rule:

---

Past: Take away the **r** and add **de**.

---

Like this:

cyklar → cykla$\not{r}$ + de → cyklade

The sentence you wanted will then look like this:

Sten cyklade igår.

Now try making the past form of the verbs in the following sentences:

| | |
|---|---|
| Olle pratar. | Olle talks. (Olle is talking.) |
| Olle städar. | Olle tidies up. (Olle is tidying up.) |
| Olle skrattar. | Olle laughs. (Olle is laughing.) |

The correct answers are, of course:

| | |
|---|---|
| Olle pratade. | Olle talked. (Olle was talking.) |
| Olle städade. | Olle tidied up. (Olle was tidying up.) |
| Olle skrattade. | Olle laughed. (Olle was laughing.) |

The problem is that not every verb follows this rule. It is only valid for verbs which end in **ar**. These verbs are called **ar** verbs. But there is another fairly large group of verbs which end in **er**, the **er** verbs. They have a somewhat different form in the past. Some change their form completely, as in the last example below:

13

| | |
|---|---|
| Olle läser. | Olle reads. (Olle is reading.) |
| Olle läste. | Olle read. (Olle was reading.) |
| Olle skriver. | Olle writes. (Olle is writing.) |
| Olle skrev. | Olle wrote. (Olle was writing.) |

Chapter 9 presents the rules for all types of verbs in Swedish. Until you have studied that chapter, you can use the rule for forming the past of **ar** verbs. When you come across a different kind of verb, you will, for the time being, have to learn the past form by heart.

If you look up a verb in a dictionary, it is usually given in the form called the *infinitive (infinitiv)*. Examples of infinitive forms of verbs in Swedish and English are: **cykla** 'cycle', **prata** 'talk', and **läsa** 'read'.

Usually the infinitive in Swedish ends in **a**. Unfortunately it is a form that is not all that useful when you are a beginner. You will probably use the present to begin with, and it is enough if you learn the verb in that form when you start to study.


## 2.2 The noun and its forms

*Noun (substantiv)* is the term for words which denote persons (**kvinna** 'woman', **pojke** 'boy'), animals (**hund** 'dog', **häst** 'horse'), things (**kniv** 'knife', **cykel** 'bicycle'), material (**vatten** 'water', **järn** 'iron'), and abstract ideas (**skönhet** 'beauty', **styrka** 'strength'). The noun has several characteristic types of endings, which we will present in Chapter 10.


## 2.3 Number

In both Swedish and English the noun has different forms for *number (numerus)*.

There are two forms which have the same name in both languages: *singular (singular)* and *plural (plural)*. In English most nouns end in **s** in the plural. In Swedish there are several different plural endings, which are used with different types of nouns. The word **stol** 'chair' forms its plural by adding **ar**: stol + ar → **stolar** 'chairs'. But **bank** 'bank' forms its plural by adding **er** : bank + er → **banker** 'banks'. There are a few other plural forms, which will be treated in detail in 10.5. To begin with you can learn the plural forms of some of the commonest nouns by heart as you come across them.

## 2.4  Definiteness

A noun in Swedish, as in English, is usually accompanied by an article. The choice between *the indefinite article (obestämd artikel)* ('a', 'an'; **en, ett**) and *the definite article (bestämd artikel)* ('the'; **-en, -et**) follows more or less the same rules in both languages. One important difference, however, is that the definite article in Swedish is an ending:

| INDEFINITE ARTICLE | | DEFINITE ARTICLE | |
|---|---|---|---|
| **en** häst | a horse | **hästen** | the horse |
| **en** katt | a cat | **katten** | the cat |

## 2.5  Gender: *en* words and *ett* words

Unlike English, the Swedish articles have different forms according to the *gender (genus)* of the nouns. Let us start with the indefinite article. In English it has two forms, but the choice between these two forms depends on the first sound of the following word, for example:

| an apple | a green apple |
|---|---|
| an egg | a brown egg |

When the following word begins with a vowel sound, you use 'an', otherwise 'a'. The indefinite article in Swedish has two forms as well. With some nouns it has the form **en** and with others the form **ett**:

| en stol | a chair | ett bord | a table |
|---|---|---|---|
| en skola | a school | ett hus | a house |
| en apelsin | an orange | ett äpple | an apple |

The choice depends not on the following sound but on the gender of the noun. Nouns which take **en** as the indefinite article are called 'en words' and those that take **ett** are called 'ett words'. As a rule you have to learn the right ending for every new noun. When you write new nouns in your note-book, write them like this:

en ban<u>a</u>n      ett äpple

The idea is that you should learn the noun together with its indefinite article, because you need to know if a noun is an **en** word or an **ett** word to be able to choose the right form of the definite article and several other grammatical points. If the indefinite article is **ett**, the definite article has a form with **t** (**et** or **t** alone) instead of a form with **n** (**en** or **n** alone):

| Sten köper **ett** äpple och **en** banan. | Sten buys an apple and a banana. |
|---|---|
| Han äter äpple**t** men inte banan**en**. | He eats the apple but not the banana. |

The way in which the indefinite and definite forms change according to whether the noun is an **en** word or an **ett** word is shown in the following table:

| 'EN' WORDS | | 'ETT' WORDS | |
|---|---|---|---|
| *Indefinite* | *Definite* | *Indefinite* | *Definite* |
| **en** banan | banan**en** | **ett** bord | bord**et** |
| a banana | the banana | a table | the table |
| **en** stol | stol**en** | **ett** kök | kök**et** |
| a chair | the chair | a kitchen | the kitchen |
| **en** gata | gata**n** | **ett** äpple | äpple**t** |
| a street | the street | an apple | the apple |

As we have already mentioned, you will normally have to learn whether each noun is an **en** word or an **ett** word. There is, however, one type of word that follows a general rule:

---

Words denoting people are **en** words.

---

Examples: **en man** 'a man', **en kvinna** 'a woman', **en pojke** 'a boy', **en flicka** 'a girl'. There is, however, one common word that is an exception to this rule: **ett barn** 'a child'.

## 2.6  Personal pronouns

The person that performs an action denoted by a verb can be shown by words like *I, you, he,* and *she*. These words are examples of what are called *personal pronouns (personliga pronomen)*. They say which person performs the action. In Swedish the verb does not change its form according to the person, so, as in English, you must always use a personal pronoun with a verb, unless there is a noun that stands as the subject and shows who performs the action.

| | |
|---|---|
| Jag arbetar. | I work. |
| Du arbetar. | You work. |
| Han arbetar. | He works. |
| Hon arbetar. | She works. |
| Vi arbetar. | We work. |
| Ni arbetar. | You work. |
| De arbetar. | They work. |

Note that the pronoun **jag** 'I' is only spelt with a capital **J** when it comes at the beginning of a sentence. As in English, the pronoun **de** 'they' is the plural of both **han** 'he' and **hon** 'she'. The pronoun **du** 'you' is nearly always used when you speak to one person, even if you do not know him or her. The pronoun **ni** 'you' can be used as a polite form of address to one person, but it is not very common to do so nowadays in Swedish. **Ni** is always used, however, when you speak to more than one person.

As in English, the pronouns **han** 'he' and **hon** 'she' are only used about people (or animals that are thought of as being more or less human). For animals and things **den** 'it' and **det** 'it' are used. **Den** is used about things which are **en** words and **det** is used about things which are **ett** words.

| | |
|---|---|
| Var är din **man?** | Where is your husband? |
| **Han** är där. | He is there. |
| Var är din **fru?** | Where is your wife? |
| **Hon** är där. | She is there. |
| Vi har **en katt.** | We have a cat. |
| **Den** heter Misse. | It is called Misse. |
| Jag köpte **ett äpple.** | I bought an apple. |
| **Det** kostade 2 kronor. | It cost 2 kronor. |
| Britta läser **en** bok. | Britta is reading a book. |
| **Den** är bra. | It is good. |
| Olle köpte **ett** paraply. | Olle bought an umbrella. |
| **Det** är svart. | It is black. |

The pronoun **de** 'they' corresponds in the plural to all the following pronouns: **han** 'he', **hon** 'she', **den** 'it', and **det** 'it'.

| | |
|---|---|
| Vad gör **Karin och Olle?** | What are Karin and Olle doing? |
| **De** spelar tennis. | They are playing tennis. |
| Sten åt **två apelsiner.** | Sten ate two oranges. |
| **De** smakade gott. | They tasted good. |
| Titta på **fåglarna!** | Look at the birds. |
| **De** är så vackra. | They are so beautiful. |

**De** is pronounced in rather a different way from what you might expect from the spelling. Usually it is pronounced **dom** (with a short 'å' sound, see 8.8). Sometimes you will see this form in writing, too, but it is thought to be rather informal:

**De** spelar tennis. = **Dom** spelar tennis.

In the following table you will find all the pronouns we have described. It is a good idea to learn them all as quickly as possible:

| SINGULAR | | PLURAL | |
|---|---|---|---|
| **jag** | I | **vi** | we |
| **du** | you | **ni** | you |
| **han** | he | | |
| **hon** | she | | |
| **den** | it (**en** words) | **de (dom)** | they |
| **det** | it (**ett** words) | | |

17

## 2.7 Adjectives

*Adjectives (adjektiv)* denote qualities, what a person or a thing is like. Some common adjectives are:

| | | | | | |
|---|---|---|---|---|---|
| **stor** | big | **ung** | young | **dyr** | dear, expensive |
| **liten** | little | **gammal** | old | **billig** | cheap |

An adjective describes a quality in a noun. It can either be put together with the noun, or after the verb **är**.

| | |
|---|---|
| Jag har en gammal bil. | I have an old car. |
| Bilen är gammal. | The car is old. |
| Du har en stor klocka. | You have a big watch. |
| Klockan är stor. | The watch is big. |

Note that, as in English, the adjective stands directly in front of the noun when it is together with it.

The adjective changes its form in a special way. This is described in Chapter 11.

## 2.8 Adverbs

*Adverbs (adverb)* are rather like adjectives, but they do not describe nouns; they qualify verbs or adjectives. In the following examples there are adverbs describing the action denoted by the verb:

| | |
|---|---|
| Lena stängde dörren **snabbt**. | Lena closed the door quickly. |
| Per läser tidningen **långsamt**. | Per reads the newspaper slowly. |

In Swedish you can often make an adverb from an adjective by adding a **t**. The adjective 'slow' is **långsam** in Swedish, and you can make an adverb from it: **långsam + t → långsamt** 'slowly'. **Snabbt** 'quickly' is formed in the same way: **snabb + t → snabbt**. The English ending **ly** as in 'slowly' and 'quickly' corresponds closely to the Swedish ending **t** as in **långsamt** and **snabbt**.

Adverbs can also qualify an adjective. Two common adverbs of this type are **mycket** 'very' and **ganska** 'rather'. In the following examples **snabb** and **långsam** function as adjectives:

| | |
|---|---|
| Lena har en mycket snabb bil. | Lena has a very fast car. |
| Per är ganska långsam. | Per is rather slow. |

## 2.9 Prepositions

*Prepositions (prepositioner)* are small words that are used a great deal in both Swedish and English. In front of a noun they show, for example, *where* or *when* something happens:

| | |
|---|---|
| Sten är **på** kontoret. | Sten is **at** the office. |
| Bilen står **på** gatan. | The car is **in** the street. |
| Eva sitter **i** bilen. | Eva is sitting **in** the car. |
| Vi bor **i** Stockholm. | We live **in** Stockholm. |
| Vi reser **i** december. | We leave **in** December. |
| Per kommer **på** onsdag. | Per is coming **on** Wednesday. |

Although quite a few Swedish prepositions have a corresponding preposition in English, it is always best to learn a preposition in a phrase:

| | |
|---|---|
| på gatan | in the street |
| på kontoret | at the office |
| i bilen | in the car |
| i december | in December |
| på onsdag | on Wednesday |

You can read more about prepositions in 15.3 and 15.4.

## 2.10 Numerals

The *numerals (räkneord)* are considered as a separate word-class. A distinction is made between *cardinal numbers (grundtal)*, which indicate number, and *ordinal numbers (ordningstal)*, which indicate order. The following are examples of cardinal numbers:

| | | | | | |
|---|---|---|---|---|---|
| 1 **en, ett** | one | | 6 **sex** | six |
| 2 **två** | two | | 7 **sju** | seven |
| 3 **tre** | three | | 8 **åtta** | eight |
| 4 **fyra** | four | | 9 **nio** | nine |
| 5 **fem** | five | | 10 **tio** | ten |

**Första** 'first' and **andra** 'second' are examples of ordinal numbers.

| | |
|---|---|
| Första maj är en helgdag i Sverige. | The first of May is a public holiday in Sweden. |

With the help of the table on the inside back cover you can form most of the numerals. It's well worth your while to try to learn all the cardinal numbers in particular as quickly as possible.

# 3 Subject, verb and object

## 3.1 The parts of a sentence

We have talked about word classes and now we must go on to look at the parts of a sentence. In Swedish a word normally belongs to a particular word class; this can be looked upon as an integral feature of a word. Words like **jägare** 'hunter' (person), **lejon** 'lion' (animal) and **gevär** 'gun' (thing) are, for example, always nouns in Swedish. Note that this distinction is not quite so clear in English. The word 'gun', for example, can be a verb as well as a noun.

But nouns can play different roles in a sentence. The following sentences have quite different meanings although they use the same nouns and the same verb:

The hunter killed the lion.
The lion killed the hunter.

You can think of these sentences as little scenes in which the nouns play different roles. These different roles are called *the parts of a sentence (satsdelar)*. The part of a sentence indicates what role a noun plays in a particular sentence, while the word class can be established for most Swedish words in isolation.

In the sentence 'The hunter killed the lion' it is the hunter that does something – he kills the lion. The person or thing that does something is called the *subject (subjekt)*. There is also someone or something that is affected by what the subject does. In the sentence above it is the lion; it gets killed. The person or thing that the subject does something to is called the *object (objekt)*. In the sentence 'The lion killed the hunter' the roles are reversed: here the lion is the subject and the hunter is the object.

You can often check what is the subject and what is the object of a sentence by asking questions. You can find the subject by asking questions like: *Who is doing (did) something? What is doing (did) something?*:

|  | *Who/What did something?* | |
|---|---|---|
| The hunter killed the lion. | The hunter | (= the subject) |
| The lion killed the hunter. | The lion | (= the subject) |
| Peter kissed Mary. | Peter | (= the subject) |
| Mary kissed Peter. | Mary | (= the subject) |

You can find the object by asking a question that contains the subject and the verb. This gives you questions like 'What did the hunter kill?', 'Who did Peter kiss?'

|  | Question | Answer (= the object) |
|---|---|---|
| The hunter killed the lion. | What did the hunter kill? | The lion. |
| Peter kissed Mary. | Who did Peter kiss? | Mary. |
| The lion killed the hunter. | Who did the lion kill? | The hunter. |
| Mary kissed Peter. | Who did Mary kiss? | Peter. |

## 3.2 Subject, object and word order in Swedish

When you make a sentence in Swedish, as in English, you normally have the word order SUBJECT + VERB + OBJECT. Don't use a different word order until you have learnt the rule that says you may do so. (You will be given several such rules later on.) To make sentences in Swedish you can use the following table:

| SUBJECT | VERB | OBJECT |
|---|---|---|
| Jägaren | dödade | lejonet. |
| The hunter killed the lion. | | |
| Lejonet | dödade | jägaren. |
| The lion killed the hunter. | | |
| Eva | skriver | ett brev. |
| Eva is writing a letter. | | |
| Olle | läser | tidningen. |
| Olle is reading the newspaper. | | |
| Familjen Nygren | äter | middag. |
| The Nygrens are having dinner. | | |
| Olle | spelar | tennis. |
| Olle is playing tennis. | | |

Some verbs only have a subject and no object. You can make this type of sentence with the same table, but the object position will be empty.

| SUBJECT | VERB | OBJECT |
|---|---|---|
| Sten | väntar. | |
| Sten is waiting. | | |
| Olle | arbetar. | |
| Olle is working. | | |
| Karin | sjunger. | |
| Karin is singing. | | |

## 3.3   Subject-verb constraint*

In Swedish, as in English, all clauses must contain a subject and a verb. This rule is called the *subject-verb constraint* or *place-holder constraint (platshållartvång)*. In many languages it is possible to leave out the subject if it is a pronoun like **I, you, we** etc., but it is not possible in Swedish:

| | |
|---|---|
| Jag sover bra. | I sleep well. |
| Vi reser hem imorgon. | We are going home tomorrow. |

In Swedish there is also, just as in English, an 'empty' subject which does not refer to anything particular. It is the pronoun **det** 'it' which is, for example, used before verbs that describe the weather:

| | |
|---|---|
| Det regnar. | It is raining. |
| Det snöar. | It is snowing. |
| Det blåser. | It is windy. |
| Det är kallt ute. | It is cold out. |
| Det är varmt inne. | It is warm indoors. |

As **det** 'it' does not refer to anything particular, it is called the *formal subject (formellt subjekt)*.

There are also languages which, in certain cases, leave out the verb, especially the verb 'be'. Here too, however, Swedish and English are alike; both languages always use a verb:

| | |
|---|---|
| Per är hungrig. | Per is hungry. |

To remind you that there must always be a subject and a verb in a Swedish sentence or clause, the subject and the verb will be marked in the tables that describe word order, like this:

| SUBJECT | VERB | OBJECT |
|---|---|---|
| Jag | kommer. | |
| I am coming. | | |
| Det | regnar. | |
| It is raining. | | |
| Vi | spelar | tennis. |
| We play tennis. | | |
| Karin | läser | tidningen. |
| Karin is reading the paper. | | |

---

* This section is mainly for those whose native language is not English.

22

# 4 *Various types of clause*

## 4.1 Clause negation: *inte*

Clauses may be affirmative clauses or negative clauses. With many verbs English uses the dummy verb 'do' + 'not' to form negative clauses. In Swedish only one word is used, **inte**, which always has the same form:

| *Affirmative clause* | *Negative clause* |
|---|---|
| Jag dricker kaffe. | Hon dricker inte kaffe. |
| I drink coffee. | She does not drink coffee. |
| Per tycker om te. | Lena tycker inte om te. |
| Per likes tea. | Lena does not like tea. |

The word **inte** is placed directly after the verb.

| SUBJECT | VERB | **inte** | OBJECT |
|---|---|---|---|
| Sten | cyklar. | | |
| Sten cycles. | | | |
| Olle | cyklar | inte. | |
| Olle does not cycle. | | | |
| Britta | äter | | frukost. |
| Britta has breakfast. | | | |
| Karin | äter | inte | frukost. |
| Karin does not have breakfast. | | | |
| Det | regnar. | | |
| It is raining. | | | |
| Det | snöar | inte. | |
| It is not snowing. | | | |

Thus it is much easier to make negative clauses in Swedish than it is in English.

## 4.2 Yes/no questions

A distinction is also made between statements and questions. A statement is used when you want to tell someone something. A question is used when you want to find out something. Depending on what kind of verb there is in the sentence, you make a question in English either by putting the dummy verb 'do' in front of the subject or by putting the auxiliary verb in front of the subject:

| *Statement* | *Question* |
|---|---|
| John likes fish. | Does John like fish? |
| You can speak Swedish. | Can you speak Swedish? |

You can answer questions like these with 'Yes' or 'No', so they are called *yes/no questions (ja/nej-frågor)*. As we saw in 1.2 there is another type of question that begins with a question word. This type is called a *question-word question (frågeordsfråga)*. We shall deal with them in the next section.

In Swedish you show that a sentence is a question simply by putting the verb at the beginning of the sentence. The subject always comes directly after the verb. No other word is needed.

| VERB | SUBJECT | OBJECT |
|------|---------|--------|
| Arbetar | Elsa? | |
| *Does Elsa work?* | | |
| Kör | hon | buss? |
| *Does she drive a bus?* | | |
| Skriver | Josefin? | |
| *Does Josefin write?* | | |
| Skriver | hon | brev? |
| *Does she write letters?* | | |
| Gillar | du | musik? |
| *Do you like music?* | | |
| Regnar | det? | |
| *Is it raining?* | | |
| Ser | du | Per? |
| *Can you see Per?* | | |

## 4.3 Question-word questions

Question-word questions are questions you cannot answer with 'Yes' or 'No'. Imagine a situation which can be described with the following sentence:

| | |
|---|---|
| Sten äter ett äpple i köket på morgonen. | Sten eats an apple in the kitchen in the morning. |

Questions and answers of the following kinds are then possible:

| *Question-word questions* | *Answers* |
|---------------------------|-----------|
| Vad gör Sten? | Han äter. |
| *What does Sten do?* | *He eats.* |
| Vem äter? | Sten. |
| *Who eats?* | *Sten.* |
| Vad äter han? | Ett äpple. |
| *What does he eat?* | *An apple.* |
| Var äter han? | I köket. |
| *Where does he eat?* | *In the kitchen.* |
| När äter han? | På morgonen. |
| *When does he eat?* | *In the morning.* |

Just as in English the question word always comes first in the sentence. But in Swedish you must always put the subject directly after the verb. No other words are needed.

Always follow the word order in the table:

| Q-WORD | VERB | SUBJECT | OBJECT |
|--------|------|---------|--------|
| Var | bor | Josefin? | |
| Where does Josefin live? | | | |
| Vad | heter | du? | |
| What is your name? | | | |
| Var | äter | Kalle | middag? |
| Where does Kalle have supper? | | | |
| När | sålde | du | bilen? |
| When did you sell the car? | | | |
| När | regnade | det? | |
| When did it rain? | | | |

Note that just as in statements there must be a subject in the question. The subject position in the table is empty only when the question word itself is the subject, as in the following questions:

| Q-WORD | VERB | SUBJECT | OBJECT |
|--------|------|---------|--------|
| Vem | bakar | | bröd? |
| Who is baking bread? | | | |
| Vad | hände? | | |
| What happened? | | | |

Note, too, that the question words do not have different forms in Swedish. The only question word that can change its form in English is 'who', which can have the form 'whom' when it is the object. But most English people use the form 'who' for subject and object, just as Swedish uses **vem**:

| | |
|---|---|
| Vem ser du? | Who (Whom) can you see? |
| Vem vet svaret? | Who knows the answer? |
| Vad är bäst? | What is best? |
| Vad köpte du? | What did you buy? |

# 4.4 Question words

The most important question words have already been described above. They are repeated in the following list, which also contains a few other, more special question words that it will pay you to learn as you come across them.

**vem** is used when you ask about a person, just like 'who' in English. **Vem** corresponds to both 'who' and 'whom'.

| | |
|---|---|
| Vem står därborta? | Who is standing over there? |
| Vem träffade du igår? | Who (Whom) did you meet yesterday? |

**vems** is used when you ask about the owner of something, just like 'whose' in English.

| | |
|---|---|
| Vems cykel lånade du? | Whose bicycle did you borrow? |

The plural of **vem** is **vilka:**

| | |
|---|---|
| Vilka kommer i kväll? | Who are coming this evening? |

**vad** is used when you ask about things. It has only one form, just like 'what' in English.

| | |
|---|---|
| Vad irriterar dig så? | What is irritating you so much? |
| Vad köpte Olle? | What did Olle buy? |
| Vad sa han? | What did he say? |

The following question words are used to ask about place:

**var** 'where'

| | |
|---|---|
| Var bor du? | Where do you live? |
| Var är tvålen? | Where is the soap? |

**vart** 'where', in the sense of 'where to'. That is, when destination and not position is referred to.

| | |
|---|---|
| Vart reste ni på semestern? | Where did you go for your holiday? |
| Vart tog han vägen? | Where did he go to? |

**varifrån** 'where . . . from'

| | |
|---|---|
| Varifrån kommer du? | Where do you come from? |

**när** 'when' is the most important question word for asking about a point in time:

| | |
|---|---|
| När tvättade du fönstren? | When did you clean the windows? |
| När dog Napoleon? | When did Napoleon die? |

**hur dags** can be used instead of **när** when you expect the answer to be clock time; in English you can ask 'What time' instead of 'When':

| | |
|---|---|
| När vaknade du imorse? | When did you wake up this morning? |
| Hur dags vaknade du imorse? | What time did you wake up this morning? |
| Klockan sju. | (At) seven o'clock. |

**varför** 'why' is used when you ask about the reason for something:

| | |
|---|---|
| Varför ljög du? | Why did you tell a lie? |
| Varför gråter Sten? | Why is Sten crying? |

**hur** 'how' is used when you ask about the way something is done:

| | |
|---|---|
| Hur kom du till Sverige? | How did you get to Sweden? |
| Hur gör man ost? | How do you make cheese? |

There are also many special question phrases that begin with **hur**:

**hur mycket** 'how much'

| | |
|---|---|
| Hur mycket kostar potatisen? | How much do the potatoes cost? |
| Hur mycket är klockan? | What time is it? |

Instead of **hur mycket** you can use **vad**:

| | |
|---|---|
| Vad kostar potatisen? | What do the potatoes cost? |
| Vad är klockan? | What is the time? |

**hur långt** 'how far'

| | |
|---|---|
| Hur långt är det till skolan? | How far is it to school? |

**hur länge** 'how long'

| | |
|---|---|
| Hur länge var du i England? | How long were you in England? |

**hur ofta** 'how often'

| | |
|---|---|
| Hur ofta går du på bio? | How often do you go to the cinema? |

**hur dags** 'when', see above.


# 4.5   Another part of the sentence: adverbials

You often want to say *where* or *when* something happens. For this you use an *adverbial (adverbial)*. Normally the adverbial comes after the object in Swedish. Do not use a different word order until you have learnt a special rule that says you may do so.

| SUBJECT | VERB | OBJECT | ADVERBIAL | |
|---|---|---|---|---|
| Britta | tvättade | bilen | i garaget. | *Var?* |
| Britta washed the car in the garage. | | | | Where? |
| Sten | cyklar | | på gatan. | *Var?* |
| Sten is cycling in the street. | | | | Where? |
| Ola | träffade | Camilla | igår. | *När?* |
| Ola met Camilla yesterday. | | | | When? |
| Vi | dricker | kaffe | efter lunch. | *När?* |
| We have coffee after lunch. | | | | When? |

Adverbials that answer the question *Where?* are called *place adverbials (platsadverbial)*, and adverbials that answer the question *When?* are called *time adverbials (tidsadverbial)*. If a sentence contains both a place and a time adverbial, the place adverbial usually comes before the time adverbial:

| | | | | ADVERBIAL | |
|---|---|---|---|---|---|
| SUBJECT | VERB | OBJECT | PLACE | TIME | |
| Britta | dricker | kaffe | i köket | på morgonen. | |

Britta has coffee in the kitchen in the morning.

| | | | | | |
|---|---|---|---|---|---|
| Jag | möter | dig | på flygplatsen | i morgon. | |

I'll meet you at the airport tomorrow.

| | | | | | |
|---|---|---|---|---|---|
| Vi | besökte | pappa | i Stockholm | i förra veckan. | |

We visited Dad in Stockholm last week.

| | | | | | |
|---|---|---|---|---|---|
| Det | regnade | i Malmö | i förrgår. | | |

It rained in Malmö the day before yesterday.

An adverbial describes various circumstances connected with the event the verb describes. There are other types of adverbial, such as phrases that answer the question *How*? These are normally placed after the object:

| SUBJECT | VERB | OBJECT | ADVERBIAL | |
|---|---|---|---|---|
| Britta | tvättade | bilen | slarvigt. | *Hur?* |

Britta washed the car carelessly.   How?

| Britta | tvättade | bilen | med en svamp. | *Hur?* |
|---|---|---|---|---|

Britta washed the car with a sponge.   How?

# 4.6  Fronting

It is quite common to begin a sentence with an adverbial instead of the subject. This is called fronting the adverbial. When the adverbial comes at the beginning of the sentence, the subject must always be placed directly after the verb, just as when question words begin a sentence (compare 4.3). In the following table the fronted part of the sentence is called X. The examples shown are based on some of the sentences in the previous section, 4.5, with the normal word order:

| X | VERB | SUBJECT | OBJECT | ADVERBIAL |
|---|---|---|---|---|
| På morgonen | dricker | Britta | kaffe | i köket. |

In the morning Britta has coffee in the kitchen.

| I köket | dricker | Britta | kaffe | på morgonen. |
|---|---|---|---|---|

The kitchen is where Britta has coffee in the morning.

| Imorse | läste | Per | tidningen | på bussen. |
|---|---|---|---|---|

This morning Per read the newspaper on the bus.

| I förrgår | regnade | det | | i Malmö. |
|---|---|---|---|---|

The day before yesterday it rained in Malmö.

| I Malmö | regnade | det | | i förrgår. |
|---|---|---|---|---|

In Malmö it rained the day before yesterday.

| Försiktigt | öppnade | Olle | dörren. | |
|---|---|---|---|---|

Carefully Olle opened the door.

As you can see from these examples, English cannot always begin a sentence with the adverbial, as Swedish can. But the main difference between Swedish and English is the word order of the subject and the verb. In Swedish the verb must come before the subject when the sentence begins with an adverbial, but not in English.

Only one adverbial can be fronted in a sentence at a time. Other parts of a sentence than an adverbial can be fronted, too, for example an object; here, too, the verb must be placed before the subject. Fronting an object is not very common and you should therefore avoid it at the beginner's stage. However, all the following variants are possible in Swedish:

**Jag köpte** den här väskan i Italien.
I Italien **köpte jag** den här väskan. } I bought this bag in Italy.
Den här väskan **köpte jag** i Italien.

## 4.7  Short answers

A yes/no question can be answered with the words 'Yes' or 'No' alone:

*Question:*    Kommer du imorgon?    Are you coming tomorrow?
*Answer:*    Ja *or* Nej.    Yes *or* No.

But in Swedish, as in English, it is quite common to add a short phrase to these answers. This kind of answer is called a *short answer* (*kortsvar*):

*Question:*    Röker han?    Does he smoke?
*Short answer:*    Ja, det gör han. *or*    Yes, he does. *or*
    Nej, det gör han inte.    No, he doesn't.

In short answers in Swedish you do not repeat the main verb in the question. Instead you use the verb **göra** 'do', in the present (**gör**) if the question is in the present, or in the past (**gjorde**) if the question is in the past. As you can see from the examples, these short answers are similar in Swedish and English:

*Question:*    Spelar hon piano?    Does she play the piano?
*Short answer:*    Ja, det gör hon. *or*    Yes, she does. *or*
    Nej, det gör hon inte.    No, she doesn't.
*Question:*    Spelade hon piano?    Did she play the piano?
*Short answer:*    Ja, det gjorde hon. *or*    Yes, she did. *or*
    Nej, det gjorde hon inte.    No, she didn't.

Note the word order in the short answers:

**Ja,**
**Nej,** + **det** + **gör** / **gjorde** + SUBJECT (+ **inte** if the answer is **nej**)

Note also how Swedish includes the word **det** 'it'. Here are a few more examples:

| | |
|---|---|
| Arbetar du här? | Do you work here? |
| – Ja, det gör jag. | – Yes, I do. |
| – Nej, det gör jag inte. | – No, I don't. |
| Arbetar de här? | Do they work here? |
| – Ja, det gör de. | – Yes, they do. |
| – Nej, det gör de inte. | – No, they don't. |
| Arbetade hon här? | Did she work here? |
| – Ja, det gjorde hon. | – Yes, she did. |
| – Nej, det gjorde hon inte. | – No, she didn't. |
| Känner du Peter? | Do you know Peter? |
| – Ja, det gör jag. | – Yes, I do. |
| – Nej, det gör jag inte. | – No, I don't. |
| Lyssnar han på radio? | Does he listen to the radio? |
| – Ja, det gör han. | – Yes, he does. |
| – Nej, det gör han inte. | – No, he doesn't. |

There are a few verbs which are not replaced by **göra** but which are repeated. The most important of these are **vara** 'be' (present: **är**, past: **var**) and **ha** 'have':

| | |
|---|---|
| Är du glad? | Are you happy? |
| – Ja, det är jag. | – Yes, I am. |
| – Nej, det är jag inte. | – No, I'm not. |
| Har han en syster? | Has he a sister? |
| – Ja, det har han. | – Yes, he has. |
| – Nej, det har han inte. | – No, he hasn't. |

Again, you can see that the Swedish and English short answers are similar.

The auxiliary verbs, which will be dealt with in 6.3, are also repeated, as in English (see 6.8).

When you answer 'Yes' to a negative question in Swedish, you use a special word, **jo**:

| | |
|---|---|
| Köpte han **inte** bilen? | Didn't he buy the car? |
| **Jo,** det gjorde han. | Yes, he did. |
| Röker han **inte**? | Doesn't he smoke? |
| **Jo,** det gör han. | Yes, he does. |

# 5   Pronouns

## 5.1   Personal pronouns

Personal pronouns have a special form when they act as the *object (objektsform):*

| | |
|---|---|
| Jag älskar **dig**. | I love **you**. |
| Älskar du **mig**? | Do you love **me**? |
| Här är Kalle. Jag ser **honom**. | Here's Kalle. I can see **him**. |
| Där är Maria. Vi ser **henne**. | There's Maria. We can see **her**. |
| De ser inte **oss**. | They can't see **us**. |
| Men vi ser **dem**. | But we can see **them**. |

In 2.6 you met the forms the personal pronouns have when they function as the subject. Here are the corresponding objective forms:

| SUBJECTIVE FORM | | OBJECTIVE FORM | |
|---|---|---|---|
| **jag** | I | **mig (mej)** | me |
| **du** | you | **dig (dej)** | you |
| **han** | he | **honom** | him |
| **hon** | she | **henne** | her |
| **den** | it (**en** words) | **den** | it |
| **det** | it (**ett** words) | **det** | it |
| **vi** | we | **oss** | us |
| **ni** | you | **er** | you |
| **de (dom)** | they | **dem (dom)** | them |

**Mig** and **dig** have special forms in spoken Swedish. You may even sometimes see them written down. These forms were given in brackets in the table above:

|  *Colloquial* | |
|---|---|
| Jag älskar dig.  = Jag älskar dej. | I love you. |
| Älskar du mig? = Älskar du mej? | Do you love me? |

In spoken Swedish, too, both **de** and **dem** have the form **dom**:

| *Colloquial* | | |
|---|---|---|
| De kommer imorgon. = Dom kommer imorgon. | They are coming tomorrow. |
| Jag ser dem. | = Jag ser dom. | I can see them. |

If you use this last form, there is no difference between the subjective and the objective forms.

In Swedish, as in English, there is only one objective form of the personal pronouns. This form is also used after prepositions and after verbs followed by a preposition:

| | |
|---|---|
| Kalle gillar Maria. | Kalle likes Maria. |
| Han talar alltid **om henne.** | He is always talking **about her.** |
| Han väntade **på henne** flera timmar. | He waited **for her** for several hours. |
| Han talade länge **med henne.** | He spoke **to her** for a long time. |
| Kalle är mycket förtjust **i henne.** | Kalle is very keen **on her.** |

## 5.2 Reflexive forms

Unlike English, which has special forms with '-self' and '-selves', such as 'myself', 'themselves', etc., Swedish uses the same objective forms of the personal pronouns as reflexives, except in the third person:

| | |
|---|---|
| Jag tvättar **mig.** | I wash myself. |
| Du tvättar **dig.** | You wash yourself. |
| Vi tvättar **oss.** | We wash ourselves. |
| Ni tvättar **er.** | You wash yourselves. |

In the third person singular and plural Swedish has a special reflexive form, **sig,** to show that the object is the same person as the subject. This form corresponds in English to 'himself', 'herself' and 'themselves':

| | |
|---|---|
| Vad gör Per? | What is Per doing? |
| Han tvättar **sig.** | He is washing (himself). |
| Vad gör Karin? | What is Karin doing? |
| Hon klär på **sig.** | She is dressing (herself). |
| Vad gör Olle och Sten? | What are Olle and Sten doing? |
| De rakar **sig.** | They are shaving (themselves). |

Compare:

| | |
|---|---|
| Vad gör du med lilla Lisa? | What are you doing with little Lisa? |
| Jag kammar **henne.** | I am combing her hair. |
| Vad gör lilla Lisa? | What is little Lisa doing? |
| **Hon** kammar **sig.** | She is combing her hair. |
| **Vi** måste skynda **oss.** | We have to hurry. |

As you can see from the examples above, many Swedish verbs which use a reflexive pronoun correspond to English verbs where there is no reflexive or where it may be left out.

The word **sig** has a special spoken form which is sometimes used in writing: **sej.**

*Colloquial*
Per tvättar sig. = Per tvättar sej.     Per is washing (himself).

The following table presents all the forms of the personal pronoun that have been discussed:

### SINGULAR

| SUBJECTIVE FORM | | OBJECTIVE FORM | | REFLEXIVE FORM | |
|---|---|---|---|---|---|
| jag | I | mig | me | mig | myself |
| du | you | dig | you | dig | yourself |
| han | he | honom | him | **sig** | himself |
| hon | she | henne | her | **sig** | herself |
| den | it | den | it | **sig** | itself |
| det | it | det | it | **sig** | itself |

### PLURAL

| SUBJECTIVE FORM | | OBJECTIVE FORM | | REFLEXIVE FORM | |
|---|---|---|---|---|---|
| vi | we | oss | us | oss | ourselves |
| ni | you | er | you | er | yourselves |
| de | they | dem | them | **sig** | themselves |

## 5.3 *man*

Another common pronoun in Swedish is **man** 'one'. It is used when you are not thinking of any particular person or when you are talking about something that concerns everybody, people in general. It can correspond in English to 'you', 'they', 'people' or 'we', as well as the more formal 'one'.

| | |
|---|---|
| Man blir trött om man sover för mycket. | One gets tired if one sleeps too much.<br>You get tired if you sleep too much. |
| I Sverige dricker man mycket kaffe. | They drink a lot of coffee in Sweden. |
| På vintern åker man ofta skidor. | In the winter people often go skiing. |
| Man ser sjön från balkongen. | One sees the lake from the balcony.<br>You can see the lake from the balcony.<br>We can see the lake from the balcony. |

The objective form of **man** is **en**. If the object refers back to the subject, the reflexive form **sig** is used:

| | |
|---|---|
| Ingen gillar **en**, om **man** skryter. | No one likes you, if you boast. |
| **Man** frågar **sig**, varför det hände. | One asks oneself why it happened. |

| SUBJECTIVE FORM | OBJECTIVE FORM | REFLEXIVE FORM |
|---|---|---|
| man 'one' | en 'one' | sig 'oneself' |

## 5.4 Word order in clauses with pronouns

In Swedish, as in English, a pronoun acting as object is always placed in the same position as a noun acting as object:

| SUBJECT | VERB | OBJECT | |
|---------|------|--------|---|
| Eva | fick | ett brev. | |
| *Eva got a letter.* | | | |
| Hon | läste | **det** | genast. |
| *She read it at once.* | | | |
| Per | känner | Maria. | |
| *Per knows Maria.* | | | |
| Han | träffade | **henne** | i London. |
| *He met her in London.* | | | |
| Erik | rakar | **sig** | varje morgon. |
| *Erik shaves every morning.* | | | |
| Jag | talade | med **dem** | på telefon. |
| *I spoke to them on the phone.* | | | |

If the clause contains the negative word **inte** 'not', however, a pronoun object is not usually placed before the **inte**. Compare:

| | |
|---|---|
| Hon läste inte brevet. | She did not read the letter. |
| Hon läste **det** inte. | She did not read it. |
| Jag såg inte Per. | I did not see Per. |
| Jag såg **honom** inte. | I did not see him. |
| Barberaren rakade inte Per. | The barber did not shave Per. |
| Per rakade **sig** inte. | Per did not shave (himself). |

A pronoun object may in certain cases come after **inte**, exactly as a noun object does. This will, however, make it contrastive and emphatic:

| | |
|---|---|
| Känner du Per? | Do you know Per? |
| Nej, jag känner inte **honom.** | No, I don't know him. |
| Men jag känner hans bror. | But I know his brother. |

# 6 Commands and clauses with more than one verb

## 6.1 Two or more verbs in succession

In English there are certain verbs that can be placed directly in front of another verb, so that you get a succession of verbs, like this:

|  | VERB$_1$ | INFINITIVE = VERB$_2$ |  |
|---|---|---|---|
| John | can | play | the piano. |
| Peter | could | sing. |  |
| Mary | must | dance. |  |

The first verb in these combinations is in the present or past. The second verb is in the form called the infinitive. Swedish has similar combinations of verbs: the first verb is, as in English, in the present or past and the second verb is in the infinitive. In Swedish the infinitive usually ends in **a**:

| SUBJECT | VERB$_1$ | INFINITIVE = VERB$_2$ |  |
|---|---|---|---|
| Jan | kan | spela | piano. |
| Jan can play the piano. |  |  |  |
| Per | kunde | sjunga. |  |
| Per could sing. |  |  |  |
| Maria | måste | dansa. |  |
| Maria must dance. |  |  |  |
| Vi | borde | arbeta. |  |
| We should work. |  |  |  |
| Du | får | röka | på balkongen. |
| You may smoke on the balcony. |  |  |  |

## 6.2 Making the infinitive from the present

In a dictionary you usually find the verbs given in the infinitive form. When you are just beginning to learn Swedish, however, you usually use the present form. So it is useful to be able to work out the infinitive form of a verb if you only know the present form. As you saw in 2.1, most verbs end in the present in **ar** or **er**:

**ar verbs**

If the verb ends in **ar** in the present, take away the **r**:

| PRESENT | Take away **r** | | INFINITIVE | |
|---------|-----------------|---|------------|---|
| öppnar | öppnaŕ | ⟶ | öppna | open |
| arbetar | arbetaŕ | ⟶ | arbeta | work |
| regnar | regnaŕ | ⟶ | regna | rain |

In the past **ar** verbs end in **ade**. If you meet this form, you can make the infinitive by taking away **de**: öppnade→ öppnad̸e̸→ öppna.

**er verbs**

If the verb ends in **er** in the present, first take away **er** and then add **a**:

| PRESENT | Take away **er** | | Add **a** | | INFINITIVE | |
|---------|------------------|---|-----------|---|------------|---|
| kommer | komm̸e̸ŕ | ⟶ | komm+a | ⟶ | komma | come |
| sover | sov̸e̸ŕ | ⟶ | sov+a | ⟶ | sova | sleep |
| köper | köp̸e̸ŕ | ⟶ | köp+a | ⟶ | köpa | buy |

The **er** verbs have various past forms, which will be presented in 9.3, 9.7 and 9.8.

## 6.3 Some common auxiliary verbs

There are a number of verbs which are used only together with another verb. They are called *auxiliary verbs (hjälpverb)*. The other verbs are called *main verbs (huvudverb)*. An auxiliary verb always comes before a main verb.

In the table below you will find some of the most important auxiliary verbs in Swedish. In the headings in bold print the infinitive is given first; then, in brackets, come the present and past forms. These verbs are very common, so it pays to learn them as quickly as possible.

**kunna (kan, kunde)** 'be able' ('can', 'could')

| | |
|---|---|
| Vi kan komma till er på söndag. | We can come to your house on Sunday. |
| Vi kan tala engelska. | We can speak English. |
| Hon kan spela tennis. | She can play tennis. |
| Hon kunde inte spela igår. | She could not play yesterday. |

**vilja (vill, ville)** 'want to' ('want to', 'wanted to')

| | |
|---|---|
| Karin vill titta på TV. | Karin wants to watch TV. |
| Men Olle vill sova. | But Olle wants to sleep. |
| Sten ville stanna hemma. | Sten wanted to stay at home. |

Note that the Swedish word **vill** does not mean 'will' in English, but corresponds to 'want to', or sometimes 'would like to'. Note also that where English uses 'want' followed by a noun as the object, the Swedish verb **vilja** is followed by **ha** + the object:

| Han vill ha kaffe. | He wants coffee. |
| Han ville ha grädde till kaffet. | He wanted cream with his coffee. |

**få (får, fick)** 'be allowed to'; 'have to' ('may', 'can', 'could')

| Du får röka, om du vill. | You may (can) smoke if you want to. |
| Hon får inte komma ikväll. | She can't (mustn't, isn't allowed to) come this evening. |
| Vi fick träffa hans fru. | We were allowed to meet his wife. *or* We got to meet his wife. |
| Hon fick vänta en timme. | She had to wait an hour. |

Note that **få** used as a main verb, with a noun as the object, means 'get', 'receive':

| Hon fick en blomma. | She got (received, was given) a flower. |
| De får alltid en present. | They always get a present. |

**– (måste, måste) –**, 'have to' ('must', 'have to', 'had to'). This verb does not have an infinitive either in Swedish or in English, and has the same form in the present as in the past.

| Du måste gå hem nu. | You must go home now. |
| Olle måste sälja bilen. | Olle must (had to) sell his car. |
| Jag måste arbeta hela kvällen igår. | I had to work the whole evening yesterday. |
| Men jag måste inte arbeta varje kväll. | But I do not have to work every evening. |

Note that English 'must not' corresponds to Swedish **får inte**:

| Du får inte röka här. | You must not smoke here. |

**skola (ska, skulle) –**, 'have to' ('shall'; 'will'; 'must', 'have to'; 'was/were going to'; 'should'; 'would'). With future meaning, see 9.2, **ska** = 'is/are going to'. In written language the form **skall** is often used instead of **ska**.

| Du ska inte göra så. | You must not (should not) do that. |
| Man ska alltid fråga honom två gånger. | You always have to ask him twice. |
| Vi skulle ha gjort det igår. | We should have done it yesterday. |
| De ska köpa ett hus på landet. | They are going to buy a house in the country. |
| Vi skulle hjälpa dig. | We were going to help you. |
| När ska vi komma? | When shall we come? |

Note that **ska (skall)** does not normally correspond to 'shall' in English.

**böra (bör, borde) –** ('should', 'ought to')

| Man bör inte dricka mer än sex koppar kaffe om dagen. | One should not drink more than six cups of coffee a day. |
| Du borde köpa en ny väska. | You ought to buy a new case. |
| De borde ha gjort det för länge sedan. | They should have (ought to have) done it long ago. |

**bruka (brukar, brukade)** – (–, used to). The English auxiliary has only one form, 'used to', in the past. **Bruka, brukar** correspond to **usually** + the main verb.

| | |
|---|---|
| Jag brukar dricka kaffe efter lunch. | I usually have coffee after lunch. |
| Josefin brukar skriva dagbok varje dag. | Josefin usually writes her diary every day. |
| Vi brukade spela kort på lördagskvällarna. | We used to play cards on Saturday evenings. |

**behöva (behöver, behövde)** 'need to' ('need to', 'needed to')

| | |
|---|---|
| Du behöver bara stanna två dagar. | You only need to stay two days. |
| Han behövde inte vänta länge. | He did not need to wait long. |

Note that, just as in English, the verb **behöva** 'need' can also be followed by a noun as the object.

| | |
|---|---|
| Jag behöver hjälp. | I need help. |

# 6.4 Commands. The imperative

If you want to tell someone to do something, you use a form of the verb called the *imperative (imperativ)*:

Come here.
Sit down.

In Swedish there is a special imperative form of the verb:

| | |
|---|---|
| Kom hit! | Come here. |
| Sätt dig! | Sit down. |

If you know the present form of an **ar** verb or an **er** verb, you can make the imperative from it.

**ar verbs**

The **ar** verbs have the same form in the imperative as in the infinitive. So you can make the imperative by taking away the **r**:

| PRESENT | Take away r | IMPERATIVE = INFINITIVE | |
|---|---|---|---|
| öppnar | öppnar | → Öppna! | open |
| lyssnar | lyssnar | → Lyssna! | listen |
| väntar | väntar | → Vänta! | wait |

**er verbs**

The **er** verbs do not have the same form in the imperative as in the infinitive. You make the imperative by taking **er** away from the present:

| PRESENT | Take away **er** | IMPERATIVE | |
|---------|---------|---------|---------|
| skriver | skriv~~er~~ | ⟶ Skriv! | write |
| känner | känn~~er~~ | ⟶ Känn! | feel |
| ringer | ring~~er~~ | ⟶ Ring! | ring |
| läser | läs~~er~~ | ⟶ Läs! | read |

Unfortunately you cannot make the imperative if you only know the infinitive of a verb, since both **ar** verbs and **er** verbs end in **a**. You cannot see from the infinitive which sort of verb it is. (But if you do know that the verb is an **er** verb, you can make the imperative by taking away the **a**. If it is an **ar** verb, you leave the **a** in the imperative.)

# 6.5   Commands, requests, and politeness phrases

If you want to be polite in English, you often use the word 'please' when you ask or tell someone to do something. Similarly in Swedish you can add the phrase **är du snäll** at the end of the sentence, or **var snäll och** at the beginning of the sentence:

| | |
|---|---|
| Köp en kvällstidning, **är du snäll.** | Buy an evening paper, please. |
| Stäng dörren, **är du snäll.** | Please close the door. |
| **Var snäll och** hämta en kudde. | Fetch a cushion, please. |

**Snäll** is an adjective which literally means 'kind', 'nice'. If you ask several people to do something, you must use the plural form **snälla** (see 11.5).

| | |
|---|---|
| Stäng dörren, **är ni snälla.** | Close the door, please. |
| **Var snälla och** stäng dörren. | Please close the door. |

Again, just as in English, it is common in Swedish not to use an imperative but to ask if someone can or could do something for you. The following questions do not expect an answer; they expect that the person you ask will do what is asked of him or her:

| | |
|---|---|
| Kan du öppna fönstret? | Can you open the window? |
| Kan du räcka mig saxen? | Can you pass me the scissors? |
| Kan Ni stänga ytterdörren? | Could you close the front door? |

# 6.6   Word order in clauses with more than one verb

The tables for word order which we have already looked at can be expanded to make room for a sequence of two or more verbs. The first verb in the table is marked with a 1: VERB$_1$. If there are any more verbs in the clause they are placed under VERB:

39

| SUBJECT | VERB₁ | VERB | OBJECT | ADVERBIAL |
|---|---|---|---|---|
| Ola | behöver | låna | pengar. | |

Ola needs to borrow money.

| SUBJECT | VERB₁ | VERB | OBJECT | ADVERBIAL |
|---|---|---|---|---|
| Jag | måste | gå | | till posten snart. |

I must go to the post office soon.

| SUBJECT | VERB₁ | VERB | OBJECT | ADVERBIAL |
|---|---|---|---|---|
| Det | börjar | regna | | nu. |

It is beginning to rain now.

| SUBJECT | VERB₁ | VERB | OBJECT | ADVERBIAL |
|---|---|---|---|---|
| Hon | måste | sluta röka | | i december. |

She must stop smoking in December.

| SUBJECT | VERB₁ | VERB | OBJECT | ADVERBIAL |
|---|---|---|---|---|
| Vi | hörde | | ett flygplan. | |

We heard a plane.

If the clause only has one verb, as in the last example, it is, of course, placed under VERB₁.

## 6.7 Sentence adverbials

There is a special group of adverbials that are placed in a different position in the clause from the other adverbials. They are called *sentence adverbials* *(satsadverbial)*. Actually **inte** 'not' (see 4.1) belongs to this group of adverbials. Others are **alltid** 'always', **ofta** 'often', **ibland** 'sometimes', **aldrig** 'never', **säkert** 'certainly', **nog** 'probably', **kanske** 'perhaps', **tyvärr** 'unfortunately', **lyckligtvis** 'fortunately', **sällan** 'seldom'.

These sentence adverbials are placed directly after VERB₁:

| SUBJECT | VERB₁ | SENTENCE ADVERBIAL | VERB | OBJECT | ADVERBIAL |
|---|---|---|---|---|---|
| Vi | vill | inte | dricka | mjölk | till maten. |

We do not want to drink milk with our food.

| SUBJECT | VERB₁ | SENTENCE ADVERBIAL | VERB | OBJECT | ADVERBIAL |
|---|---|---|---|---|---|
| Du | måste | alltid | skriva | postnummer | på alla brev. |

You must always write the postal code on all letters.

| SUBJECT | VERB₁ | SENTENCE ADVERBIAL | VERB | OBJECT | ADVERBIAL |
|---|---|---|---|---|---|
| Det | brukar | aldrig | snöa | | i augusti. |

It very rarely snows in August.

| SUBJECT | VERB₁ | SENTENCE ADVERBIAL | VERB | OBJECT | ADVERBIAL |
|---|---|---|---|---|---|
| Alla | behöver | inte | sova | | åtta timmar. |

Not everybody needs to sleep eight hours.

| SUBJECT | VERB₁ | SENTENCE ADVERBIAL | VERB | OBJECT | ADVERBIAL |
|---|---|---|---|---|---|
| Olle | reser | sällan | | | utomlands. |

Olle seldom travels abroad.

| SUBJECT | VERB₁ | SENTENCE ADVERBIAL | VERB | OBJECT | ADVERBIAL |
|---|---|---|---|---|---|
| Vi | träffade | ofta | | Per | i Stockholm. |

We often met Per in Stockholm.

As we saw when we dealt with clauses containing only one verb, the verb comes before the subject in yes/no questions (see 4.2), in question-word questions (4.3) and with fronting (4.6). In clauses with more than one verb it is VERB$_1$ that is placed before the subject. The next few sections deal with the word order in this kind of clause. To make it easier for you to see the pattern we will not specify the parts of the sentence that follow the sentence adverbial. They are not affected, and follow the same word order as in the table above.

## 6.8 Yes/no questions with more than one verb

When you make a question that can be answered 'Yes' or 'No' (a yes/no question, 4.2), VERB$_1$ is placed at the beginning of the sentence and is followed directly by the subject:

| VERB$_1$ | SUBJECT | SENTENCE ADVERBIAL | |
|----------|---------|--------------------|--|
| Vill | ni | inte | dricka mjölk till maten? |

Don't you want to drink milk with your food?

| Kan | du | | börja jobba på måndag? |
|-----|----|--|------------------------|

Can you start work on Monday?

| Måste | flickan | | komma tillbaka imorgon? |
|-------|---------|--|-------------------------|

Does the girl have to come back tomorrow?

| Brukar | de | | stanna i Sverige på sommaren? |
|--------|----|--|-------------------------------|

Do they usually stay in Sweden in the summer?

| Känner | du | | Sven? |
|--------|----|--|-------|

Do you know Sven?

| Regnar | det | ofta | på sommaren? |
|--------|-----|------|--------------|

Does it often rain in the summer?

In *short answers* (4.7) the auxiliary verb is repeated. It cannot be replaced by **göra.**

| **Kan** du simma? | Can you swim? |
|-------------------|---------------|
| – Ja, det **kan** jag. | – Yes, I can. |
| – Nej, det **kan** jag inte. | – No, I can't. |
| **Vill** hon spela? | Does she want to play? |
| – Ja, det **vill** hon. | – Yes, she does. |
| – Nej, det **vill** hon inte. | – No, she doesn't. |

## 6.9 Question-word questions and fronting with more than one verb

The rules for question-word questions and for fronting can be combined in one rule. The table showing the word order is then as follows:

| X or QUESTION WORD | VERB$_1$ | SUBJECT | SENTENCE ADVERBIAL | |
|---|---|---|---|---|
| Imorgon | måste | du | | komma i tid. |
| Tomorrow you must be on time. | | | | |
| Här | får | du | inte | röka. |
| You mustn't smoke here. | | | | |
| Förr | ville | Sten | alltid | titta på TV hela kvällen. |
| Sten always used to want to watch TV all evening. | | | | |
| Vad | vill | ni | | göra imorgon? |
| What do you want to do tomorrow? | | | | |
| Hur dags | får | jag | | ringa? |
| What time can I phone? | | | | |
| Vem | kan | jag | | fråga? |
| Who can I ask? | | | | |
| Vem | kan | | inte | simma? |
| Who can't swim? | | | | |
| Vad | hände | | | på festen i fredags? |
| What happened at the party on Friday? | | | | |

You can only leave the subject position empty when the question word is the subject, as in the last two questions.

# 7 Complex sentences

As we saw in 1.3, a sentence can consist of one or more clauses. A sentence that consists of only one clause is called a *simple sentence (enkel mening)*. A sentence that consists of two ore more clauses is called a *complex sentence (sammansatt mening)*. The first two sentences below consist of only one clause; they are simple sentences. The remaining three sentences are complex sentences.

| | |
|---|---|
| Per sjunger. | Per sings. |
| Lotta spelar dragspel. | Lotta plays the accordion. |
| Per sjunger och Lotta spelar dragspel. | Per sings and Lotta plays the accordion. |
| De säger, att Per sjunger. | They say that Per sings. |
| De säger, att Per sjunger och att Lotta spelar dragspel. | They say that Per sings and that Lotta plays the accordion. |

In previous chapters we have seen how simple sentences consisting of only one clause are made. In this chapter we shall show how complex sentences are made by joining simple sentences together in various ways.

## 7.1 Coordination and subordination

Two clauses can be joined together by **och** 'and'. This is called *coordination (samordning)*:

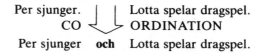

The clauses that are coordinated by **och** are equal. One clause can also be included in another clause, so that it becomes a part of the other clause. This is called *subordination (underordning)*. In the following example the clause **Per brukar äta vitlök** 'Per usually eats garlic' is subordinated by being introduced by **att** 'that':

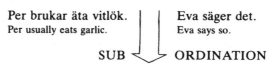

The clause introduced by **att** acts as the object of the verb **säger** 'says' in the same way as **det** does in the first example. Compare the examples in the following table showing word order:

| SUBJECT | VERB | OBJECT |
|---------|------|--------|
| Eva | säger | det. |
| Eva | säger, | att Per brukar äta vitlök. |

## 7.2 Main clause and subordinate clause

A distinction is also made between main clauses and subordinate clauses. A clause that is part of another clause is called a *subordinate clause* or a *subclause (bisats)*. A subordinate clause can never make a sentence by itself. A clause which is independent and is not part of another clause is called a *main clause (huvudsats)*. A clause that makes a sentence by itself is always a main clause:

| MAIN CLAUSE | MAIN CLAUSE |
|-------------|-------------|
| Per sjunger. | Per sings. |

A sentence must always contain at least one main clause. If you coordinate two main clauses, they are still main clauses:

MAIN CLAUSE                    MAIN CLAUSE

Per sjunger                och        Lotta spelar dragspel.
Per sings and Lotta plays the accordion.

If you use subordination, one clause is changed into a subordinate clause. The clause that the subordinate clause is part of is the main clause. The example given in 7.1 is built up in the following way:

MAIN CLAUSE

Eva säger, att Per brukar äta vitlök.

SUB-CLAUSE

If you coordinate two subordinate clauses with **och** 'and', they remain subclauses:

MAIN CLAUSE

Eva säger, att Per sjunger och att Lotta spelar dragspel.

SUB-CLAUSE            SUB-CLAUSE

There are several different kinds of subordinate clauses. The most important of them will be described in the following sections.

## 7.3  *Att* clauses

Subordinate clauses that begin with **att** are called *att clauses (att-bisatser)*. They usually act as the object of verbs like **säga** 'say', **veta** 'know', **tro** 'think', **se** 'see' and **höra** 'hear':

| | |
|---|---|
| Mannen sa, att han var trött. | The man said that he was tired. |
| Jag tror, att Elsa kommer hit ikväll. | I think that Elsa will come here this evening. |
| Alla vet, att chefen kom för sent imorse. | Everyone knows that the boss was late this morning. |
| Vi såg nog, att du gäspade. | We saw that you yawned alright. |
| Jag hör, att någon startar en bil. | I can hear that someone is starting a car. |

As in English, you can leave out the word **att** 'that', but not always. You can do so, for example, in the first two sentences above:

| | |
|---|---|
| Mannen sa han var trött. | The man said he was tired. |
| Jag tror Elsa kommer hit ikväll. | I think Elsa will come here this evening. |

But it is never wrong to include **att**, so it is simplest to do so if you are not sure which is best.

In Swedish you can put a *comma (kommatecken)* (,) before an **att** clause, provided that **att** is not omitted. However, the comma is not obligatory. Usually the comma is omitted if the **att** clause is relatively short, as in the examples above. We have included the comma, however, to show where it may be placed.

## 7.4  Adverbial clauses

Subordinate clauses can also act as adverbials. These clauses are called *adverbial clauses (adverbialsbisatser)*. It is easy to recognize adverbial clauses by their opening word. The commonest words that open adverbial clauses are:

**när** 'when'

| | |
|---|---|
| Mamman vaknade när barnet började gråta. | The mother woke up when the child began to cry. |

**innan** 'before'

| | |
|---|---|
| Karin gör läxorna innan hon äter middag. | Karin does her homework before she has supper. |

**medan** 'while'

| | |
|---|---|
| Du kan läsa tidningen medan jag duschar. | You can read the paper while I have a shower. |

**om** 'if'

| | |
|---|---|
| Jag går hem om Lisa kommer hit. | I'll go home if Lisa comes here. |

**därför att** 'because'

| | |
|---|---|
| Olle grät, därför att Ville hade retat honom. | Olle cried because Ville had teased him. |

**eftersom** 'since', 'as'

| | |
|---|---|
| Vi badade inte, eftersom vattnet var förorenat. | We didn't bathe as (since) the water was polluted. |

**fastän** 'although', 'though'

| | |
|---|---|
| Olle somnade i soffan, fastän familjen tittade på TV. | Olle fell asleep on the sofa although the family was watching TV. |

**trots att** 'although', 'in spite of the fact that'

| | |
|---|---|
| Vi gav oss iväg, trots att det regnade. | We set off although (in spite of the fact that) it was raining. |

Adverbial clauses can be placed in a word-order table. They come in the same place as other adverbials:

| SUBJECT | VERB | OBJECT | ADVERBIAL |
|---|---|---|---|
| Jag | träffade | Lisa | imorse. |

I met Lisa this morning.

| SUBJECT | VERB | OBJECT | ADVERBIAL |
|---|---|---|---|
| Jag | träffade | Lisa | när jag handlade mat. |

I met Lisa when I was doing the food shopping.

| SUBJECT | VERB | OBJECT | ADVERBIAL |
|---|---|---|---|
| Jag | betalar | bensinen | om du skjutsar mig hem. |

I'll pay for the petrol if you give me a lift home.

| SUBJECT | VERB | OBJECT | ADVERBIAL |
|---|---|---|---|
| Olle | somnade | | i soffan, fastän familjen tittade på TV. |

Olle fell asleep on the sofa although the family was watching TV.

Adverbial clauses can be placed first in the sentence just like other adverbials (see 4.6). Note that the subject must come after the verb in the main clause, in exactly the same way as when an ordinary adverbial is placed at the front of the sentence:

| X | VERB | SUBJECT | OBJECT | ADVERBIAL |
|---|---|---|---|---|
| Imorse | träffade | jag | Lisa. | |

This morning, I met Lisa.

| X | VERB | SUBJECT | OBJECT | ADVERBIAL |
|---|---|---|---|---|
| När jag handlade mat, | träffade | jag | Lisa. | |

When I was doing the food shopping, I met Lisa.

| X | VERB | SUBJECT | OBJECT | ADVERBIAL |
|---|---|---|---|---|
| Om du skjutsar mig hem, | betalar | jag | bensinen. | |

If you give me a lift home, I'll pay for the petrol.

| X | VERB | SUBJECT | OBJECT | ADVERBIAL |
|---|---|---|---|---|
| Fastän familjen tittade på TV, | somnade | Olle | | i soffan. |

Although the family was watching TV, Olle fell asleep on the sofa.

46

A comma can be placed both before and after an adverbial clause in Swedish, if it is necessary for the sake of clarity. The comma is often omitted in these cases, too. We have included the comma in the examples above merely to show where it may be placed. The comma is not obligatory.

Note that the subject can never be left out after the subordinators listed above:

| | |
|---|---|
| Eva gick till jobbet, trots att **hon** var förkyld. | Eva went to work in spite of having a cold. |
| När jag gick längs gatan, träffade jag min vän Per. | Walking along the street I met my friend Per. |

## 7.5 Word order in subordinate clauses

The word order in a subordinate clause is in certain respects different from the word order in a main clause. This is particularly true of the position of sentence adverbials (compare 6.7). Sentence adverbials are always placed before the verb in a subordinate clause. Compare the following examples in which the same clause appears first as a main clause and then as a subordinate clause:

| | |
|---|---|
| Sten vill **inte** sova. | Sten doesn't want to sleep. |
| Olle säger, att Sten **inte** vill sova. | Olle says that Sten doesn't want to sleep. |
| Per kommer **alltid** för sent. | Per is always late. |
| Vi väntar inte på Per, eftersom han **alltid** kommer för sent. | We won't wait for Per as he is always late. |
| De slutar **inte** sjunga. | They don't stop singing. |
| Jag blir arg, om de **inte** slutar sjunga. | I'll get angry if they don't stop singing. |

In English sentences the sentence adverbials have the same position in both main and subordinate clauses, so it is important to remember that the word order is not the same in Swedish: sentence adverbials in subordinate clauses always come *before* the verb in Swedish.

Also, the subject always comes before the verb in a subordinate clause. Here it is not possible to put any other part of a sentence before the subject. However, as we have seen, subordinate clauses usually begin with an opening word called a *subordinator (bisatsinledare)*. The following table shows how the word order in a subordinate clause differs from the word order in a main clause:

| SUBORD-INATOR | SUBJECT | SENTENCE ADVERBIAL | VERB$_1$ | (the rest as in a main clause) |
|---|---|---|---|---|
| Olle säger, att | Sten | inte | vill | sova. |

Olle says that Sten does not want to sleep.

| | | | | |
|---|---|---|---|---|
| Camilla säger, att | hon | | kan | spela tennis. |

Camilla says that she can play tennis.

| | | | | |
|---|---|---|---|---|
| Ola säger, att | han | inte | kan | spela tennis. |

Ola says that he cannot play tennis.

| | | | | |
|---|---|---|---|---|
| Jag vet, att | de | alltid | reser | till fjällen på vintern |

I know that they always go up to the mountains in the winter.

| | | | | |
|---|---|---|---|---|
| Per tippar, trots att | han | aldrig | vinner. | |

Per does the pools although he never wins.

| | | | | |
|---|---|---|---|---|
| Vi kommer, om | vi | inte | måste | jobba över. |

We'll come if we do not have to work overtime.

| | | | | |
|---|---|---|---|---|
| Alla gillar Eva, eftersom | hon | ofta | skojar | om allting. |

Everybody likes Eva as she often jokes about everything.

## 7.6  Relative clauses

There is also a type of sub-clause that tells you more about a noun. This is called a *relative clause (relativbisats)*. Relative clauses in English are mostly introduced by 'who', 'which' or 'that'. In Swedish they are introduced by **som**. This word never changes its form:

| | |
|---|---|
| Sten har en syster, **som** bor i Malmö. | Sten has a sister who lives in Malmö. |
| Lasse känner en kvinna, **som** arbetar på DN. | Lasse knows a woman who works at DN. |
| Stig har en papegoja **som** talar. | Stig has a parrot that talks. |
| Ann har två dockor, **som** är sönder. | Ann has two dolls which are broken. |

Relative clauses are described in greater detail in 16.7.

# 8   Pronunciation and spelling

Pronunciation and spelling have already been described briefly in 1.1.

## 8.1   Vowels and consonants

The sounds of all languages are divided into two major groups: *vowels (vokaler)* and *consonants (konsonanter)*. The vowels can be sub-divided into vowels and diphthongs. A *diphthong (diftong)* is a combination of two vowel sounds. In standard British English there are 12 vowels, 9 diphthongs and 24 consonants.

Many of these sounds do not have their own letters. Instead they are represented by combinations of letters, like **th, ch, oy** and other special spelling patterns.

The Swedish language has 9 vowels and 18 consonants; it does not have any diphthongs, except in certain dialects.

| *Vowels* | *Consonants* |
|---|---|
| i e ä y ö o å a u | p t k b d g s sj tj h |
| | f v j l r m n ng |

Several of the consonant sounds in Swedish do not have a letter of their own. They are spelt by using a combination of several letters which is read as one sound. This will be explained later on.

In Swedish, as in English, you can often hear from a person's pronunciation where he or she comes from. Pronunciation varies from one part of the country to another. In the following we shall mainly describe the pronunciation in Stockholm and central Sweden.

## 8.2   How sounds in language are made. Voiced and voiceless sounds

To understand the difference between vowels and consonants you need to know something about the ways in which the sounds in a language are made. These sounds are formed when air passes from the lungs through the larynx, the throat and the mouth. In the larynx the air passes through a narrow passage. The edges of this passage form the vocal chords. If the vocal chords are brought towards each other, they are caused to vibrate by the air from the lungs. This creates a vocal tone. You can test this out on yourself by saying a longdrawn *aaaaa*. If you put two fingers on your larynx, you will be able to feel the vibrations. Sounds made with a vocal tone are called *voiced sounds (tonande ljud)*. The opposite of voiced is *voiceless (tonlös)*, that is sounds without a vocal tone. All vowels are voiced. Consonants, however, can be divided into voiced consonants and voiceless consonants. You can test the difference by saying a long-drawn *vvvvv* and a long-drawn *sssss*. If you put two fingers on your larynx, you will feel that *v* is voiced (vibrations) and that *s* is voiceless. (Be careful not to say a vowel at the same time. Don't say *ess*.)

The most important difference between vowels and consonants is that air can pass freely through the windpipe and mouth when you say a vowel sound, while there is a constriction or closing somewhere when you say a consonant. You notice this most clearly when the 'block' is at the lips. Say the consonant *p*, for example in the word *paper*. Notice how the lips close completely for an instant when you say the *p*'s and open when you say the vowels *a* and *e*. You can try looking in a mirror at the same time.

## 8.3   Length and stress

In 1.1 we pointed out that Swedish distinguishes between long and short vowels in pronunciation. English does not have the same clear distinction, though the words *hit* and *heat* can be said to have a short and a long *i* sound respectively.

The spelling of short and long vowels in Swedish is not very consistent. A single vowel (letter) is used in writing both when the vowel is pronounced long and when it is pronounced short. To make it easier for you to pronounce the Swedish words we will use a special marking system. A dash (_) is placed under the long vowels and a dot (.) under the short ones. These marks are not used in ordinary written texts in Swedish:

| *Normal text* | | *Marked text* |
|---|---|---|
| tal | speech | ta̱l |
| tall | pine | ta̤ll |
| rik | rich | ri̱k |
| risk | risk | ri̤sk |

The words in the examples above have only one vowel. But many words have more than one vowel, which creates another difficulty in Swedish: *stress (betoning)*. Stress means that you say one part of a word with more emphasis than the rest. In Swedish it is usually the first vowel that is *stressed (betonad)*, but as in English there are also quite a few words which do not follow this rule. One example is the word **banan** 'banana'. As in English, the first vowel is not stressed but the second one is, though this is, of course, not indicated by the spelling.

There is a connection between stress and length in Swedish:

A stressed vowel may be either long or short.
An unstressed vowel is always short.

50

This means that we can use the marks for long and short vowels to show where a word is stressed. With the words that have been marked for pronunciation the marks for long and short vowels have only been used under the stressed vowel. If a vowel is not marked it is unstressed and short. Normally one and only one vowel is stressed in a word. If a word only has one vowel, it is automatically stressed, when the word is said in isolation. The usual rule is that the first vowel in a word is stressed, but there are quite a few exceptions to this rule. Many are words that have been borrowed from other languages, such as French.

Here are some examples of words with different lengths and stress patterns. First, some examples of words with the stress on the first vowel:

| vila | rest | villa | house |
| silar | strainers | sillar | herrings |

And here are some words with the stress not on the first vowel:

| magasin | warehouse | tablett | tablet | teater | theatre |
| paket | packet | metall | metal | | |
| betona | stress | försök | try | behålla | keep |

Here are some words which are very similar in English and Swedish, where the stress is on the first vowel in English but not in Swedish:

| Italy | Italien |
| telephone | telefon |
| formal | formell |

# 8.4  Acute and grave accent

In Swedish pronunciation there is another feature which has no equivalent in English. It is the difference between what are called the *acute* and the *grave* accent (*akut accent, grav accent*). Certain words differ only in the accent they have, for example:

| *Acute accent* | | *Grave accent* | |
| anden | the duck | anden | the spirit |
| stegen | the steps | stegen | the ladder |
| vaken | the hole in the ice | vaken | awake |

The stress is on the same vowel in these pairs of words, but they are pronounced with different 'tunes', which mark the only difference between them. This difference is quite difficult to hear if Swedish is not your native language. It may help you to think of the acute accent as being the usual tone, with a low falling tone on the second syllable. The grave accent has a higher falling tone on the second syllable, rather like the way you say *side* in the word *offside*. In fact, there are very few cases where you will be misunderstood if you use the wrong accent. So you can wait until a more advanced level to learn the two accents.

## 8.5 Swedish long vowels

Here is a complete list of the long vowels in Swedish. The comparisons with English refer to British English.

i is pronounced more or less as the vowel sound in *bee, mean*, but a little more closed:

vin    wine        vila    rest

e is pronounced as French *é*:

te    tea        leka    play

ä is somewhat like the sound in *men*, but longer:

läsa    read        häl    heal

y is pronounced rather like the French *u* or the German *ü*:

ny    new        lysa    shine

ö is pronounced rather like the French *eu* in *peu*:

öl    beer        dö    die

o is pronounced rather like the *oo* in *school*:

ros    rose        sol    sun

å is rather like the *ou* in *ought*, though closer:

år    year        låna    borrow

a is pronounced like the *a* in *father*, though a little further back in the mouth:

vara    be        ja    yes

u is a difficult sound to pronounce correctly. Keep your lips close together.

hus    house        mur    wall

Some points to note:

**i/y** The difference between these two sounds is that *y* is pronounced with the lips rounded. Make a long *i* sound and then round your lips and you will get the *y* sound. Ask someone who speaks Swedish to pronounce *i* and *y* one after the other and see how the lips move. Look in a mirror when you practise saying these sounds yourself.

**e/ö** These two sounds differ in the same way as *i* and *y*. Make a long *e* sound and round your lips and you will get the *ö* sound.

Note that the long vowels *i, y, u* and *o* finish with a consonant-like sound:

bi    bee        by    village        bu!    boo!        bo    live

People who are not native speakers of Swedish can easily confuse words like **bo** 'live' and **bov** 'villain'.

## 8.6 Swedish short vowels

Apart from being shorter, of course, certain of the Swedish short vowels differ from the corresponding long ones in special ways.

**u̲ ụ** The biggest difference is between long and short *u*. Try to hear the difference and repeat the following pairs of words:

| bu̲s | bụss |
|------|------|
| mischief | bus |
| hu̲s | hụnd |
| house | dog |
| ru̲sa | rụsta |
| rush | arm (with weapons) |
| slu̲ta | slụtta |
| stop | slope |

**ẹ = ạ̈** In most parts of Sweden there is no difference between the vowels *e* and *ä* when they are pronounced short. Both of them are pronounced very like the sound in *bed*. There are even certain words that are pronounced exactly the same although they are spelt in different ways:

| sẹtt | sạ̈tt |
|------|------|
| seen | way, manner |

There are no other special differences between the long and short pronunciations of the other vowels:

| i̲ | ị | vịn | vịnn |
|----|---|-----|------|
|    |   | wine | win |
| y̲ | ỵ | sỵl | sỵlt |
|    |   | awl | jam |
| ö̲ | ọ̈ | fọ̈l | fọ̈ll |
|    |   | foal | fell |
| o̲ | ọ | rọt | rọtt |
|    |   | root | rowed |
| å̲ | ạ̊ | hạ̊l | hạ̊ll |
|    |   | hole | direction |
| a̲ | ạ | hạt | hạtt |
|    |   | hate | hat |

Note that the short ạ does not have the *å* quality of the long a̲.

Note, too, that the short vowels keep their distinct pronunciations even when they are unstressed and are not reduced to *e*.

| heder | honour | flickor | girls |
|-------|--------|---------|-------|
| hedar | heaths | pojkar | boys |
| redo | ready, prepared | gäster | guests |
| rede | nest | hästar | horses |
| reda | order | | |

## 8.7 Pronunciation of *ö* and *ä* before *r*

The vowels *ö* and *ä* are pronounced in a special way when they come before an *r*. This special sound may be marked with a small raised *r*, thus: ö$^r$, ä$^r$. You can hear a clear difference between these sounds and an ordinary *ö* or *ä* in the following:

| ö̠ | ö̠$^r$ | hö̠ | hö̠r |
|----|------|-----|-----|
|    |      | hay | hear |
| ọ̈ | ọ̈$^r$ | dọ̈tt | dọ̈rr |
|    |      | died | door |
| ä̠ | ä̠$^r$ | hä̠l | hä̠r |
|    |      | heel | here |
| ạ̈ | ạ̈$^r$ | mạ̈tt | mạ̈rr |
|    |      | full-up | mare |

In particular you should practise recognizing the sounds ö$^r$ and ä$^r$ when you listen to Swedish. It is not particularly disturbing, on the other hand, if you use an ordinary *ö* and *ä* in your own pronunciation. In fact, in certain parts of Sweden this is the pronunciation you will hear.

Note that a short *ä* sound is pronounced in this special way even when it is spelt with an **e**. (As mentioned in 8.6 the *e* sound and the short *ä* sound are pronounced the same.) Thus the first vowel in the following word is pronounced as *ä* although it is spelt with an **e**:

hẹrre        lord, master

## 8.8 Pronunciation of the letter *o*

The letter **o** can cause problems in Swedish. The sound *o* is always spelt with this letter. But the trouble is that the sound *å* is also spelt with the letter **o** in certain words. In particular a short *å* sound is often spelt in this way. So when you learn a word with the short *å* sound, you must make sure to learn whether it is spelt with the letter **å** or the letter **o**. All the following words are pronounced with a short *å* sound although the spelling varies:

| *å* sound | lọpp | race |
|-----------|------|------|
|           | mạ̊tt | measurement, size |
|           | jọbb | job |

A short *o* sound is actually rather unusual in Swedish, so you may reasonably suppose that the letter **o** will be pronounced as a short *å* sound. The words which in fact have a short *o* sound are, however, spelt with the letter **o**, for example **ost** 'cheese'.

Because of these difficulties you should always pay special attention to the pronunciation of a word which is spelt with the letter **o**. There are the following possibilities:

| Letter | Sound | | | |
|---|---|---|---|---|
| o — o | sol | sun | (Normal) |
| — å | lov | holiday | (Exception) |

o < 
- o    ost    cheese    (Few Swedish words are pronounced with a short *o*.) (Normal spelling of the short *o*.)
- å    jobb    job    (Normal spelling of the short *å* sound.)

Compare:

hov (o) hoof      hov (å) court      håv (å) bag net
kol (å) coal      kål (å) cabbage
kort (o) card      kort (å) short

The letter å never causes any trouble. It is always pronounced as an *å* sound.

## 8.9 Swedish consonants

All consonants are formed by the air which passes through the windpipe and emerges at the mouth being obstructed at some point (see 8.2). Consonants differ from each other in three different ways:

- The obstacle to the passage of air can occur at different points.
- The passage of air may be obstructed in different ways.
- Some consonants are voiced and others are voiceless (8.2).

We shall look particularly closely here at two groups of consonants. They are the *stops* and the *fricatives*. The latter group comprises several sounds that are difficult to learn.

## 8.9.1 Swedish stops

When you say a stop, the stream of air is completely blocked for an instant. That is what happens when you say a *p* in the word *ape*. You close your lips when you say a *p*. (You can check this by looking in a mirror.) Other stops are *t* and *k*. They are different from *p* because the blockage occurs at another point. When you say *t*, you raise the tip of your tongue to a point just behind your top front teeth; when you say *k* the back of your tongue is raised and touches your soft palate so that the stream of air is checked for an instant.

Swedish has the following stops:

| Voiceless | p | t | k |
|---|---|---|---|
| Voiced | b | d | g |

Just as in English, the stops in the top and bottom row are paired off, as the stream of air is blocked at the same point. The difference is that the upper stop in each pair is voiceless, while the lower one is voiced (8.2). These sounds are all pronounced almost identically in Swedish and English. One slight difference is that *t* and *d* in Swedish are pronounced with the tongue against the back of the upper front teeth, not as in English with the tongue just above the front teeth.

## 8.9.2 Swedish fricatives

When you say a fricative, the stream of air passes through a narrow opening, which makes a kind of hissing sound. But the opening is not so narrow as to stem the air stream completely.

The Swedish fricatives are:

| Voiceless | **f** | **s** | **sj** | **tj** |
|-----------|-------|-------|--------|--------|
| Voiced | **v** | | | |

As you can see, Swedish does not have the voiced equivalents of *s, sj* and *tj* as English has. Thus there is no *z* sound in Swedish as there is in English words like *busy, nose.* Nor does Swedish have the *th* fricatives of English words like *thing* and *that.*

*f, v* and *s* have identical pronunciations in English and Swedish, and so cause no trouble.

The letter combination **s + j** in Swedish is pronounced as one sound. The same is true of the combination **t + j**.

The sound represented by *sj* is rather like the English *sh* sound in *shop,* but is formed further back in the mouth with the lips more rounded. This sound is also spelt **sk, skj, stj, sch** or **ch** (see 8.12–8.13).

The sound represented by *tj* is the voiceless counterpart of the Swedish *j,* which is very similar to the *y* in the English word *young* (see 8.10). It can be made by saying a long-drawn Swedish *j,* but suppressing the voicing to make the sound voiceless (see 8.2). It is a little like the English *ch* sound in *church* without the *t* sound at the beginning. It may also be spelt **k, kj**.

It is important in Swedish to keep the two sounds *sj* and *tj* separate. It is the difference between these sounds that constitutes the difference between the following words (note that there is only one consonant sound before the first vowel):

| | | | |
|---|---|---|---|
| skjuta | tjuta | skära | tjära |
| shoot | howl | cut | tar |
| chock | tjock | skälla | källa |
| (ch is pronounced | fat | bark | source |
| as sj) | | skön | kön |
| shock | | lovely | sex |

56

## 8.10 Other consonants

The other consonants in Swedish do not cause much trouble. They are very nearly identical with the same consonants in English:

| | | | |
|---|---|---|---|
| **m** | mat | food | |
| | mäta | measure | |
| **n** | natt | night | |
| **ng** | säng | bed | The letter combination **ng** is always pronounced in Swedish as in the English word *singer* and not as in *finger*. |
| | sång | song | |
| | finger | finger | |
| **h** | ha | have | |
| | hamn | harbour | |
| **j** | ja | yes | The *j* sound is normally pronounced like the *y* sound in the English word *yes*. |
| | jo-jo | yo-yo | |
| **l** | lära | learn | The Swedish *l* is always pronounced like the *l* sound in the English word *love,* and never as in the words *milk, well* etc. |
| **r** | röd | red | The Swedish *r* is usually slightly rolled, like the Scottish *r*. In the south of Sweden a special burred *r* is used. Note that Swedish *r* at the end of words has the same sound as at the beginning of words. It is not dropped as in British English words like *car, doctor*. |

## 8.11 Consonant combinations

As well as learning to pronounce single consonant sounds you will also have to learn to pronounce various combinations of consonants. There are quite a few of them, as Swedish, just like English, can have two or even three consonant sounds before a vowel. When there are three consonants, the first one is always **s**, as in **strand** 'beach'.

Note that **k** and **g** are always pronounced before an **n** at the beginning of a word:

| | |
|---|---|
| knä | knee |
| knacka | knock |
| gnaga | gnaw |

After a vowel **gn** is pronounced **ng + n**:

| | |
|---|---|
| vagn | carriage |
| lugn | calm |

## 8.12 Letters combined with *j* pronounced as one sound

We saw in 8.9.2 that the letter combinations **sj** and **tj** are pronounced as one sound. There are some other combinations that are pronounced in the same way; all of them end in the letter **j**. In addition there are certain combinations consisting of a consonant + **j** in which the first letter is not pronounced. These combinations are therefore pronounced as **j**:

| *Letter combination* | *Sound* | *Example* | |
|---|---|---|---|
| dj | | djup | deep |
| gj | j | gjorde | did |
| hj | | hjälpa | help |
| lj | | ljus | light |
| sj | | sjuk | sick |
| stj | sj | stjärna | star |
| skj | | skjorta | shirt |
| tj | tj | tjock | fat |
| kj | | kjol | skirt |

In words borrowed from other languages there are also a few letter combinations which are pronounced *sj* or *tj*:

| *sj* | *tj* |
|---|---|
| sch: schack, schema | – |
| sh: sherry, shoppa | – |
| ch: chock, chef, chaufför, chans | check, charter |

The many loan words which end in **-tion** and **-sion**, are pronounced as if they were spelt **-sjon**:

| station | station |
|---|---|
| lektion | lesson |
| diskussion | discussion |

In a few words a *t* is heard before the *sj* sound in **-tion: nation** 'nation', **motion** 'exercise'.


## 8.13 Pronunciation of the letters *g*, *k* and *sk* before front vowels

Vowels can be divided into two groups, called front vowels and back vowels, in the following way. (The terms refer to the highest point on the back of the tongue when saying the vowel.)

| *Front vowels* | *Back vowels* |
|---|---|
| i e ö ä y | o å a u |

When the letters **g**, **k** and **sk** come before a front vowel, they are not pronounced in the usual way. Instead, the letter **g** is pronounced *j* as in **ja**, the letter **k** *tj* as in **tjugo** and the letters **sk** *sj* as in **sjunga**.

| Letter | Sound | Example | |
|--------|-------|---------|--|
| g | j | ge | give |
|   |   | göra | do, make |
| k | tj | kyla | cold (noun) |
|   |   | köra | drive |
| sk | sj | skina | shine |
|   |   | skön | lovely |

Before a back vowel these letters are pronounced in the usual way.

Note that after **r** and **l** the letter **g** is pronounced as *j*:

| rg → rj | berg | mountain | torg | market square |
|---------|------|----------|------|---------------|
| lg → lj | helg | public holiday | | |

## 8.14 Pronunciation of the consonant combinations *rt*, *rd*, *rn* and *rs*

In central and northern Sweden the letter **r** combined with certain other letters is pronounced as one sound. One example of this kind of combination is **r + t**. In a word like **borta** 'away', for example, **rt** is pronounced as one sound. If you are a beginner you need not worry too much about pronouncing this sound; **rt** pronounced in the ordinary way will not lead to misunderstanding and does, in fact, occur in certain parts of the country. The biggest problem is to hear the sound that occurs in such words when **rt** is pronounced as one sound. The same is true of the other combinations, **rd**, **rn** and **rs**, and also of the combination **rl**, which is, however, not very common.

So practise listening to the difference between the following pairs of words:

| fat | – | fart |
|-----|---|------|
| saucer | | speed |
| bod | – | bord |
| shed | | table |
| ton | – | torn |
| tone | | tower |
| mos | – | mors |
| pulp | | mother's |

The same pronunciation also occurs when a word ends in **r** and the next word begins with one of the consonants **t**, **d**, **n** or **s**. In the following short sentences you will see examples of this. A little link is placed between **r** and the consonant which are pronounced as one sound.

| **rt** | Han dricker te. | He is drinking tea. |
| **rd** | Förstår du? | Do you understand? |
| **rn** | Har ni tid? | Have you got time? |
| **rs** | Du kommer för sent. | You are too late. |

## 8.15 Doubled consonants

As we have seen, the length of vowels is not given by the spelling in Swedish. But for consonants it is. The basic rule is:

---

A doubled consonant is pronounced as a long consonant sound.

---

As well as there being a difference between long and short vowels, there is also a difference between long and short consonants, as in the following examples:

| hat | – hatt | sil | – sill | rys | – ryss |
| hate | hat | strainer | herring | shudder | Russian (noun) |

Long consonants are not at all common in English and only occur between two words, for example: 'black coffee', 'good dog'; but they are very common in Swedish.

One peculiarity of Swedish spelling is that the letter **k** is not doubled. Instead **ck** is used:

lack     varnish         tacka     thank

---

**ck** replaces **kk**.

---

The pronunciation of long and short consonants does not usually cause any great difficulty. Also, the difference between a long and a short vowel is very much more important than the difference between a long and a short consonant. In Swedish a long vowel cannot come directly before a long consonant; it can only come before a short consonant. So you can usually work out from the spelling whether a vowel should be pronounced long or short. There is one condition: that you know whether the vowel is stressed or not. So the following rules apply only to words that contain one vowel only, since if there is only one vowel it must be stressed (when the word is pronounced in isolation. See 8.3):

| | Ordinary text | Marked text |
|---|---|---|
| A vowel is pronounced as a long vowel | | |
| if the vowel is stressed and | | |
| a) not followed by a consonant | bi | bi̱ |
| b) followed by only one consonant | bil | bi̱l |
| A vowel is pronounced as a short vowel if | | |
| a) it is followed by a double consonant | Bill | Bi̱ll |
| b) it is followed by two or more consonants | bild | bi̱ld |
| c) it is unstressed, as is the second vowel | | |
| in this word | bilda | bi̱lda |

If a word has only one vowel, you can tell from the spelling whether the vowel is long or short. The problem is that you cannot be sure where the stress is in a word which has more than one vowel. As the stress is usually on the first vowel in Swedish, you can guess that the first vowel is stressed and then use the rules given above. If you want to be certain, you will have to look the word up in a book which marks the stress, or ask someone who knows how it is pronounced. So it pays dividends to note down new words and mark the length and stress. In certain cases you can work out that the stress is not on the first vowel when there is more than one vowel in a word. If a consonant is doubled, the vowel directly before it will normally be stressed and short. Compare the following words:

| fo̱rmel | forme̱ll | hote̱ll |
|---|---|---|
| formula | formal | hotel |

Note also the following rule:

---
Adding an ending does not normally change length and stress.
---

Compare the following words:

| va̱ls | va̱ls (va̱l + s) |
|---|---|
| waltz | of an election |
| sva̱ns | sva̱ns (sva̱n + s) |
| tail | of a swan |

# 8.16 Doubling of *m* and *n*

There are special rules for the doubling of **m** and **n**.

---
The letter **m** is doubled only between two vowels.
---

Otherwise only one **m** is written, even if it is long and comes directly after a short stressed vowel. If a word ends in a stressed vowel + **m**, the vowel is sometimes pronounced long, and sometimes short:

| *Between two vowels* | | *At the end of a word* | |
|---|---|---|---|
| komma | come | Kom! | Come! |
| rummet | the room | ett rum | a room |
| But: | | | |
| damen | the lady | en dam | a lady |

Note that this rule means that there is an unexpected change in the spelling of certain words when they have an ending. This is not reflected in a change of pronunciation. For **n** note that:

---

**The letter n is not doubled at the end of a few very common words.**

---

| (Han) kan | (He) can | *But:* kunna | be able to |
|---|---|---|---|
| en man | a man | *But:* mannen | the man |
| en | one; a, an | | |

han, hon, den   he, she, it   (Personal pronouns, 5.1.)
min, din, sin   my, your, his/her   (Possessive pronouns, 12.2.)
nån, sån   (Informal spoken forms of **någon** and **sådan**, see 13.3 and 13.5.)

There are a few more words like this.

Note also that **n** is never doubled before **d** and **t**:

| känt | known | *But:* känna | know |
|---|---|---|---|
| kände | knew | *But:* känns | feel(s) |

In other respects **n** follows the main rule.

## 8.17 Capital and small letters

In Swedish, capital letters are used in the same way as in English, with a few exceptions:

All nationality words in Swedish, unlike English, begin with a small letter. Nationality words are used as the names of languages, as adjectives and to talk about people from a certain country or a nation as a whole:

| Hur många av er kan tala | How many of you can speak |
|---|---|
| engelska, tyska eller franska? | English, German or French? |
| Min mamma är finsk, men min | My mother is Finnish, but my |
| pappa är svensk. | father is Swedish. |

| I den här stadsdelen bor det många greker. | A lot of Greeks live in this part of town. |

Names of the days of the week, months and seasons also begin with a small letter:

| Vi reser till fjällen på fredag. | We are going to the mountains on Friday. |
| I Stockholm börjar vintern ofta inte förrän i december, men i norra Sverige börjar den redan i slutet av oktober. | In Stockholm winter often does not come until December, but in northern Sweden it comes as early as the end of October. |

The first word in names of films, plays and books begins with a capital letter, but not, as in English, any of the other words:

| Filmen som vi såg i går heter Gudarna måste vara tokiga. | The film we saw yesterday is called "The Gods Must Be Mad". |

# 9 The verb and its forms

## 9.1 The perfect and the pluperfect

The present and the past were described in 2.1. These tenses are formed by changing the ending of the verb. As in English, there are also tenses which are formed by using an auxiliary verb. In both Swedish and English there is a *perfect tense (perfekt)* and a *pluperfect tense (pluskvamperfekt)*:

| PERFECT | PLUPERFECT |
|---|---|
| Jag **har varit** sjuk.<br>I have been ill. | Jag **hade varit** sjuk.<br>I had been ill. |
| Per **har badat.**<br>Per has had a bath. | Per **hade badat.**<br>Per had had a bath. |
| Eva **har rest** utomlands.<br>Eva has gone abroad. | Eva **hade rest** utomlands.<br>Eva had gone abroad. |

Swedish forms the perfect and the pluperfect in the same way as English, with forms of the verb 'have', which functions as an auxiliary in these constructions (compare 6.3). The main verb also changes its form to what is called the *supine (supinum)*:

Per har öppnat fönstret.       Per has opened the window.
Per hade öppnat fönstret.       Per had opened the window.

The rules for forming the perfect and the pluperfect are thus:

> Perfect:   **har** + supine

Jag har läst annonsen.       I have read the advertisement.
Vi har frågat Ann.       We have asked Ann.

> Pluperfect:   **hade** + supine

Jag hade läst annonsen.       I had read the advertisement.
Vi hade frågat Ann.       We had asked Ann.

The perfect and pluperfect tenses have almost identical uses in Swedish and English. One slight difference, however, is that the perfect tense in Swedish is sometimes used to describe an action in the past where English uses the past tense.

| | |
|---|---|
| Det har regnat i natt. | It rained last night. |
| Strindberg har skrivit många pjäser. | Strindberg wrote many plays. |

# 9.2 The future

As in English there is no obvious *future tense (futurum)* in Swedish. Instead there are a number of ways that are used to show that something will happen in the future. Future time is denoted by the auxiliary verbs **kommer att** or **ska** followed by the main verb in the infinitive, or by the present tense.

FUTURE

| | |
|---|---|
| Sven kommer att resa hem. | Sven will go home. |
| Sven ska resa hem. | Sven is going to go home. |
| Kerstin kommer att sälja bilen. | Kerstin will sell the car. |
| Kerstin ska sälja bilen. | Kerstin is going to sell the car. |
| Det kommer att regna imorgon. | It will (is going to) rain tomorrow. |
| Jag ska öppna fönstret. | I'll open the window. |

There is a certain difference between these two types of future. The **kommer att** construction is the basic one. It denotes a pure prediction or assumption about what will be happening in the future. **Ska** is used mainly when the wishes (or intentions) of the subject or some other person affect what will happen. Compare the following examples, which are appropriate for somewhat differing situations:

| | |
|---|---|
| Alla kommer att vara här klockan 5. | Everbody will be here at 5 o'clock. (I think.) |
| Alla ska vara här klockan 5. | Everybody is to be here at 5 o'clock. (We have decided.) |
| Sven kommer att dö ung. | Sven will die young. (He has such poor health. Prediction) |
| Sven ska dö ung. | Sven is going to die young. (Said by a gunman. Threat.) |

If it is a question of something that the subject of the verb is planning or intends to do, the verb **tänker** + the infinitive is often used as an alternative to **ska**:

| | |
|---|---|
| Vi tänker flyga hem. | We are going to fly home. |
| Vi ska flyga hem. | We'll fly home (We are going to fly home.) |

If the context clearly shows that future time is meant, it is often possible to use the present in Swedish. The same is true of English, though mainly with certain verbs like 'come', 'go', 'see' etc.

| | |
|---|---|
| Vi reser till fjällen på lördag. | We're going to the mountains on Saturday. |
| Det regnar säkert imorgon. | It will certainly rain tomorrow. |
| Jag är inte här nästa vecka. | I won't be here next week. |

Thus future time may be expressed in Swedish in the following ways:

---

Future:
**kommer att** + infinitive (prediction about the future)
**ska** + infinitive (the wish of the subject or someone else)
**tänker** + infinitive (the subject's wish)
present (the time is given by the context)

---

The following table gives a rough comparison of the ways in which Swedish and English express future time:

| | |
|---|---|
| **kommer att** | = will |
| **ska** | = is going to (is to) |
| **tänker** | = is going to |
| present | = present continuous (will) |

Learning the exact shades of meaning of the various ways of expressing the future in Swedish takes time. The description given above is not enough on its own to enable you to decide which form to use.

When you come across sentences that contain a future form, try to work out why that particular form has been chosen rather than another in that particular situation.

## 9.3 How to make the verb forms

We have now, in various places in the book, discussed five forms which a verb can have. The problem is that different kinds of verbs make these forms in somewhat different ways. Here is a table of all the forms we have discussed:

| | IMPERATIVE | INFINITIVE | PRESENT | PAST | SUPINE |
|---|---|---|---|---|---|
| **ar** verbs | öppna! | öppna | öppnar | öppnade | öppnat |
| | open! | open | open(s) | opened | opened |
| | fråga! | fråga | frågar | frågade | frågat |
| | ask! | ask | ask(s) | asked | asked |

| | IMPERATIVE | INFINITIVE | PRESENT | PAST | SUPINE |
|---|---|---|---|---|---|
| **er** verbs | ring! | ringa | ringer | ringde | ringt |
| | ring! | ring | ring(s) | rang | rung |
| | känn! | känna | känner | kände | känt |
| | feel! | feel | feel(s) | felt | felt |
| | köp! | köpa | köper | köpte | köpt |
| | buy! | buy | buy(s) | bought | bought |
| | läs! | läsa | läser | läste | läst |
| | read! | read | read(s) | read | read |

The present is the form you will use most, so it is natural to begin by learning the present form of the verb. But later, when you are able to make use of several different forms of a verb, it is easiest to make them by always starting with the imperative. This is what we shall do from now on. If you come across a verb in the present, you can always make the basic form with the aid of the rules given in 6.4. Take away the **r** in **ar** verbs (öppna/r → öppna) and the **er** in **er** verbs (ring/er → ring).

---

The imperative = the basic form

---

If you remember that the imperative is the basic form, you do not need to know anything else about the verb, not even whether it is an **ar** verb or an **er** verb. You can always work that out. **Ar** verbs end in an **a** in the imperative, while **er** verbs end in a consonant. In the rules that follow our only point of reference will be the form of the verb in the imperative.

## 9.4 The infinitive

The *infinitive (infinitiv)* ends in **a**. If the basic form already has an **a** (**öppna**, **fråga**) no ending is added. If the basic form ends in a consonant, an **a** is added.

| BASIC FORM | | INFINITIVE | |
|---|---|---|---|
| öppna | | ⟶ öppna | open |
| fråga | | fråga | ask |
| ring | + a | ⟶ ringa | ring |
| känn | + a | känna | know (a person); feel |
| köp | + a | köpa | buy |
| läs | + a | läsa | read |

The rule for forming the infinitive is thus:

---

Infinitive:   basic form + **a**
(No ending is added if the basic form ends in **a**.)

---

## 9.5 The supine

The *supine (supinum)* is formed by adding **t** to the basic form.

| BASIC FORM | | | SUPINE | |
|---|---|---|---|---|
| öppna | + t | ⟶ | öppnat | opened |
| fråga | + t | | frågat | asked |
| ring | + t | ⟶ | ringt | rung |
| känn | + t | | känt | known (a person); felt |
| läs | + t | | läst | read |
| köp | + t | | köpt | bought |

The rule for forming the supine is thus:

---

Supine:   basic form + **t**

---

The supine is the form of the verb used with the auxiliary 'have' to make the perfect and pluperfect tenses. This function corresponds to one of the functions of the past participle in English (compare 9.15).

## 9.6 The present

There are two endings in the *present (presens)*: **r** and **er**. If the basic form ends in **a**, add an **r**. Otherwise, add **er**. (In this case the basic form always ends in a consonant.)

| BASIC FORM | | | PRESENT | |
|---|---|---|---|---|
| öppna | + r | ⟶ | öppnar | open(s) |
| fråga | + r | | frågar | ask(s) |
| ring | + er | ⟶ | ringer | ring(s) |
| känn | + er | | känner | know(s); feel(s) |
| köp | + er | | köper | buy(s) |
| läs | + er | | läser | read(s) |

The rule for forming the present is thus:

---

Present:  basic form + **r** after **a**
          basic form + **er** after a consonant

---

## 9.7 The past

The *past (preteritum)* has the endings **de** and **te**. The ending **te** is used if the basic form ends in a voiceless consonant. Otherwise **de** is used (after the vowel **a** which is a voiced sound and after voiced consonants). Voiceless consonants are **p, t, k** and **s**. If the basic form ends in one of these consonants, use **te**. Otherwise use **de**.

| BASIC FORM | | PAST | |
|---|---|---|---|
| öppna | + de | → öppnade | opened |
| fråga | + de | frågade | asked |
| ring | + de | → ringde | rang |
| känn | + de | kände | knew; felt |

The basic form ends in a voiceless consonant:

| BASIC FORM | | PAST | | |
|---|---|---|---|---|
| köp | + te | → köpte | bought | p |
| byt | + te | bytte | changed | t |
| rök | + te | rökte | smoked | k |
| läs | + te | läste | read | s |

The rule for forming the past is thus:

---
Past:  basic form + **de**
       basic form + **te** after voiceless consonants (p, t, k, s)

---

## 9.8 Strong verbs

Some **er** verbs have special forms in the past and the supine which you will have to learn by heart. These verbs are called *strong verbs (starka verb)*. They change their vowel in the past and usually in the supine, too. Here are a few strong verbs in all their forms:

| IMPERATIVE = BASIC FORM | INFINITIVE | PRESENT | PAST | SUPINE |
|---|---|---|---|---|
| spring! run! | springa run | springer run(s) | sprang ran | sprungit run |
| sitt! sit! | sitta sit | sitter sit(s) | satt sat | suttit sat |
| skriv! write! | skriva write | skriver write(s) | skrev wrote | skrivit written |
| skin! shine! | skina shine | skiner shine(s) | sken shone | skinit shone |
| sjung! sing! | sjunga sing | sjunger sing(s) | sjöng sang | sjungit sung |

Only **er** verbs can be strong verbs; **ar** verbs never are. The infinitive and the present follow the rules for all **er** verbs. As the basic form ends in a consonant, the verb has an **a** in the infinitive and **er** in the present.

In the past there is no ending. Instead, the vowel is changed:

spring!        sprang
run!             ran

sjung!        sjöng
sing!             sang

In the supine the vowel changes only in some of the strong verbs. But they all have a special supine ending: **it**. (Other verbs only have a **t**.)

sprung**it**    run      sjung**it**    sung      skriv**it**    written

As you can see, many of the Swedish strong verbs correspond to strong verbs in English, with somewhat similar changes of form.

As the infinitive and the present can be formed according to a simple rule, there is no need to learn these by heart. But learn the other three forms by heart. These three forms are called *the principal parts* of the verb (verbets *tema*). In the following you will find the principal parts of the most important strong verbs. The vowel changes follow three definite patterns, which have been placed above the principal parts. It is easiest to remember the verb forms if you learn verbs with similar forms in a group together.

| IMPERATIVE = BASIC FORM | PAST | SUPINE | |
|---|---|---|---|
| 1. **i** | **a** | **u** | |
| bind! | band | bundit | bind |
| brinn! | brann | brunnit | burn |
| drick! | drack | druckit | drink |
| finn! | fann | funnit | find |
| försvinn! | försvann | försvunnit | disappear |
| hinn! | hann | hunnit | manage, have time to |
| rinn! | rann | runnit | run, flow |
| sitt! | satt | suttit | sit |
| slipp! | slapp | sluppit | get out of |
| sprick! | sprack | spruckit | split |
| spring! | sprang | sprungit | run |
| stick! | stack | stuckit | stick, sting |
| vinn! | vann | vunnit | win |
| 2. **i** | **e** | **i** | |
| bit! | bet | bitit | bite |
| grip! | grep | gripit | grip |
| lid! | led | lidit | suffer |
| rid! | red | ridit | ride |
| skin! | sken | skinit | shine |

70

| IMPERATIVE = BASIC FORM | PAST | SUPINE | |
|---|---|---|---|
| skriv! | skrev | skrivit | write |
| slit! | slet | slitit | wear out, tear |
| stig! | steg | stigit | rise |
| tig! | teg | tigit | be silent |
| vrid! | vred | vridit | turn |
| 3. u/y | ö | u | |
| bjud! | bjöd | bjudit | invite |
| ljug! | ljög | ljugit | lie, tell a lie |
| sjung! | sjöng | sjungit | sing (Note, short vowels.) |
| skjut! | sköt | skjutit | shoot |
| bryt! | bröt | brutit | break |
| flyg! | flög | flugit | fly |
| flyt! | flöt | flutit | float, flow |
| frys! | frös | frusit | freeze, be cold |
| knyt! | knöt | knutit | tie up |
| kryp! | kröp | krupit | crawl, creep |

| Infinitive: | basic form + **a**: bind**a**, bit**a**, bjud**a**, bryt**a** |
|---|---|
| Present: | basic form + **er**: bind**er**, bit**er**, bjud**er**, bryt**er** |

## 9.9 Short verbs

**Ar** and **er** verbs in their basic forms end in an unstressed **a** and a consonant respectively. There is a third possibility. Certain verbs in their basic form end in a long, stressed vowel. These verbs are very short; they normally consist of the long vowel preceded by only one or two consonants:

Ge! Give!     Se! See!     Tro! Believe!

The present tense form is also short. Add an **r** and you have the present:

ger    give(s)     ser    see(s)     tror    believe(s)

So these verbs can be called the *short verbs* (*kortverb*). Below you will find first the regular short verbs. For them it is enough to learn the basic form; you can then make the other forms according to the rules. But there is also another group of short verbs which are irregular in the past. Some of the commonest verbs are in this group, so it is worth learning these forms as quickly as possible. They are given immediately after the regular short verbs below:

| IMPERATIVE =BASIC FORM | INFINITIVE | PRESENT | PAST | SUPINE | |
|---|---|---|---|---|---|
| tro! | tro | tror | tro**dde** | tro**tt** | believe, think |
| ske! | ske | sker | ske**dde** | ske**tt** | happen |
| nå! | nå | når | nå**dde** | nå**tt** | reach |
| bo! | bo | bor | bo**dde** | bo**tt** | live |
| må! | må | mår | må**dde** | må**tt** | feel (of health) |
| klä | klä | klär | klä**dde** | klä**tt** | dress |

*Short verbs with an irregular past*

| | | | | | |
|---|---|---|---|---|---|
| (få!) | få | får | **fick** | få**tt** | get, receive |
| gå! | gå | går | **gick** | gå**tt** | go, walk |
| ge! | ge | ger | **gav** | ge**tt** | give |
| se! | se | ser | **såg** | se**tt** | see |
| dö! | dö | dör | **dog** | dö**tt** | die |
| stå! | stå | står | **stod** | stå**tt** | stand |
| be! | be | ber | **bad** | be**tt** | ask, pray |

A short verb ends in a long, stressed vowel in the imperative and the infinitive. The present is formed by adding an **r**:

---

Present: basic form + **r**

---

The past is formed by adding **dde**. Note that the long vowel is now short.

---

Past: basic form + **dde**

---

The supine is formed by adding **tt**. Here, too, the vowel is shortened:

---

Supine: basic form + **tt**

---

## 9.10 Irregular verbs

There are also some verbs that do not follow any rules (or where the rule only applies to one or two verbs, so it is not worth learning). Some of these verbs are like the strong verbs, others are like the short verbs. **Ar** verbs, however, are always regular.

The most important irregular verbs are given below:

| IMPERATIVE =BASIC FORM | INFINITIVE | PRESENT | PAST | SUPINE | |
|---|---|---|---|---|---|
| var! | vara | är | var | varit | be |
| ha! | ha | har | hade | haft | have |
| kom! | komma | kommer | kom | kommit | come |
| gör! | göra | gör | gjorde | gjort | do, make |
| ta! tag! | ta | tar | tog | tagit | take |
| säg! | säga | säger | sa, sade | sagt | say |
| vet! | veta | vet | visste | vetat | know |
| låt! | låta | låter | lät | låtit | let |
| håll! | hålla | håller | höll | hållit | hold |
| (het!) | heta | heter | hette | hetat | be called |
| far! | fara | far | for | farit | go |
| bär! | bära | bär | bar | burit | carry |
| dra! drag! | dra | drar | drog | dragit | pull, drag |
| ligg! | ligga | ligger | låg | legat | lie (down) |
| lägg! | lägga | lägger | la, lade | lagt | put |
| sätt! | sätta | sätter | satte | satt | put |
| slå! | slå | slår | slog | slagit | hit |
| fall! | falla | faller | föll | fallit | fall |
| ät! | äta | äter | åt | ätit | eat |
| sov! | sova | sover | sov | sovit | sleep |
| stjäl! | stjäla | stjäl | stal | stulit | steal |
| gråt! | gråta | gråter | grät | gråtit | cry |
| *j verbs* | | | | | |
| sälj! | sälja | säljer | sålde | sålt | sell |
| välj! | välja | väljer | valde | valt | choose |
| vänj! | vänja | vänjer | vande | vant | accustom |
| svälj! | svälja | sväljer | svalde | svalt | swallow |
| skilj! | skilja | skiljer | skilde | skilt | separate |

# 9.11 The passive

As we have already seen, the subject often indicates who does something. When the person who does something is unknown or not identified, a special form of the verb is often used which is called the *passive (passiv)*. The ordinary verb form is called the *active form (aktiv form)* indicating that the subject is active and carries out the action which the verb describes:

| ACTIVE FORM | PASSIVE FORM |
|---|---|
| Per opens the door. | The door **is opened.** |
| Lisa broke the window. | The window **was broken.** |

The passive in Swedish is formed simply by adding an **s** to the verb. (The next section describes in detail how the forms are made.) As in English, the passive can be used when the subject is unknown or not identified. In Swedish a passive sentence often has the same meaning as an active sentence using **man** 'one' (5.3). In English 'one' and 'you' are often used in the same way. Other possible unidentified subjects in Swedish are **någon** 'somebody' and **de** 'they':

| ACTIVE FORM | PASSIVE FORM |
|---|---|
| Någon stängde dörren. <br> Somebody closed the door. | = Dörren stängdes. <br> The door was closed. |
| Man kan stänga dörren med en nyckel. <br> You can close the door with a key. | = Dörren kan stängas med en nyckel. <br> The door can be closed with a key. |
| Man måste stryka skjortan. <br> You must iron the shirt. | = Skjortan måste strykas. <br> The shirt must be ironed. |
| Man informerar oss aldrig. <br> They never inform us. | = Vi informeras aldrig. <br> We are never informed. |
| Man har reparerat lägenheten. <br> They have repaired the flat. | = Lägenheten har reparerats. <br> The flat has been repaired. |

As in English, you can also use the passive when the person who does something is known. The person is then introduced by the preposition **av** 'by':

| ACTIVE FORM | PASSIVE FORM |
|---|---|
| Per öppnade dörren. <br> Per opened the door. | = Dörren öppnades av Per. <br> The door was opened by Per. |
| Värden har reparerat lägenheten. <br> The landlord has repaired the flat. | = Lägenheten har reparerats av värden. <br> The flat has been repaired by the landlord |

Passive constructions are not the first ones that you need to use when you speak and write yourself, but it is important for you to be able to understand them. They are often used, for example, in simple instructions and notices:

| | |
|---|---|
| Öppnas här. | To be opened here. (Open here.) |
| Bör förbrukas senast 24.12. | Should be used by 24.12. |
| Får ej vidröras. | Not to be touched. (Do not touch.) |

## 9.12 Making the *s* form of verbs

The **s** form of verbs is very simple. You just add an **s** to the other endings of the verb. The only special point to remember is that the present tense ending **r** disappears before the **s**:

öppna~~r~~ + s → öppnas
ge~~r~~   + s → ges

If the present ends in **er**, usually the whole ending disappears:

köp~~er~~ + s → köps
sälj~~er~~ + s → säljs

If you like, you can leave the **e** in, and you will then have the form that is mainly used in more formal, written Swedish:

köpe~~r~~ + s → köpes
sälje~~r~~ + s → säljes

Here are all the **s** forms of the verb **räkna** 'count':

| | | | | |
|---|---|---|---|---|
| INFINITIVE | räkna | + s → | räknas | be counted |
| PRESENT | räkna~~r~~ | + s → | räknas | am/is/are counted |
| PAST | räknade | + s → | räknades | was/were counted |
| SUPINE | räknat | + s → | räknats | been counted |

Kassan räknas varje kväll. — The money in the till is counted every evening.

Igår räknades den tre gånger. — Yesterday it was counted three times.

Den har aldrig räknats så noggrant. — It has never been counted so carefully.

There are a few verbs which always have the **s** form without having a passive function. They are listed with this form in word lists and dictionaries. Among the commonest are:

**hoppas (hoppas, hoppades, hoppats)** 'hope'

Alla hoppas, att de kommer att vinna. — Everybody hopes they will win.

**minnas (minns, mindes, mints)** 'remember'

Jag minns inte hans namn. — I don't remember his name.

**trivas (trivs, trivdes, trivts)** 'enjoy life', 'get on'

Per trivs på jobbet. — Per enjoys his work.

# 9.13 The participle forms of the verb

Apart from the forms that have already been presented, the verb also has two participle forms: the *present participle (presens particip)* and the *past participle (perfekt particip)*. The participles can be used in the same way as adjectives (see Chapter 11):

PRESENT PARTICIPLE

en **läsande** pojke
a reading boy

en pojke som läser
a boy who reads/is reading.

en **skrattande** kvinna
a laughing woman

en kvinna som skrattar
a woman who laughs/is laughing

## PAST PARTICIPLE

| | |
|---|---|
| en **stängd** dörr<br>a closed door | en dörr som någon har stängt<br>a door that someone has closed |
| en **betald** räkning<br>a paid bill | en räkning som man har betalat<br>a bill that one has paid |

When the verb is formed with a particle (see 9.17) the particle is placed directly before the participle to make one word:

| | |
|---|---|
| **stänga av** 'turn off' | **avstängd** 'turned off' |
| **springa bort** 'run away' | **bortsprungen** 'run away' |
| en avstängd TV<br>a turned-off TV | en TV som man har stängt av<br>a TV one has turned off |
| en bortsprungen hund<br>a stray dog | en hund som har sprungit bort<br>a dog that has run away |

The prefix **o** before the participle has the meaning 'not' or 'un'.

| | |
|---|---|
| en oläst bok<br>an unread book | en bok som man inte har läst<br>a book that one has not read |
| en obetald räkning<br>an unpaid bill | en räkning som man inte har betalat<br>a bill that one has not paid |

In English the present participle can also be used as an adjective as in Swedish; but Swedish does not use the present participle as English does in sentences such as:

He wrote a letter saying he was ill.

Here Swedish uses two main verbs:

Han skrev ett brev och talade om att han var sjuk.

In Swedish the past participle is not used after the auxiliary verb 'have' to form the perfect and the pluperfect tenses. As you saw in 9.5, the supine is used for this purpose.

In 9.11 we pointed out that when the English past participle, preceded by a form of the verb 'be', is used in the passive construction, the usual equivalent in Swedish is a passive construction with the s form of the Swedish verb. Actually, the past participle can be used in Swedish, too, after the verbs **vara** 'be' and **bli** 'become'. In general, **bli** + past participle stresses the action and **vara** + past participle the result:

| | |
|---|---|
| Bilen blev reparerad, medan vi väntade.<br>Bilen reparerades, medan vi väntade. | The car was repaired while we waited. |
| Bilen var reparerad, när vi kom tillbaka.<br>Bilen hade reparerats, när vi kom tillbaka. | The car was repaired when we returned. |

| | |
|---|---|
| Presidenten blev skjuten av en lejd mördare. | The president was shot by a hired assassin. |
| Presidenten sköts av en lejd mördare. | |
| Villan är redan såld. | The house is already sold. |
| Villan har redan sålts. | The house has already been sold. |

## 9.14 The present participle

To make the present participle, begin with the same basic form as for other verb forms, the imperative. The present participle ends in **ande** except when the basic form ends in a long, stressed vowel, in which case **ende** is used. Verbs that end in an unstressed a lose this in front of **ande**; for example **öppna** 'open': öppn𝑎 + ande → öppnande.

BASIC FORM     PRESENT PARTICIPLE

arbet𝑎 + ande  → arbetande     working
(*Note:* the **a** in the basic form disappears.)

häng   + ande  → hängande     hanging
läs    + ande     läsande        reading
spring + ande     springande     running
gå     + ende  → gående        walking, going
tro    + ende     troende        believing

The rules can be summed up:

---

Present participle: basic form + **ande**
                      basic form + **ende** after a long stressed vowel

---

## 9.15 The past participle

The past participle is made from the basic form by adding **d, t** or **dd; d** is added to verbs that end in **a** or a voiced consonant in the basic form:

BASIC FORM     PAST PARTICIPLE

intressera + d  → intresserad     interested
öka      + d     ökad          increased
glöm     + d     glömd         forgotten
stäng    + d     stängd        closed

**t** is added to verbs that end in a voiceless consonant (**p, t, k, s**):

BASIC FORM     PAST PARTICIPLE

| | | | |
|---|---|---|---|
| köp | + t | → köpt | bought |
| tänk | + t | tänkt | thought |
| läs | + t | läst | read |

**dd** is added to verbs that end in a long, stressed vowel (= short verbs):

BASIC FORM     PAST PARTICIPLE

| | | | |
|---|---|---|---|
| tro | + dd | → trodd | believed |
| klä | + dd | klädd | dressed |

The past participle of strong verbs is made in a special way. These verbs always end in **en** in the past participle. Also, the vowel changes in the same way as in the supine. To make the past participle of a strong verb, you start with the supine, take away **it** and add **en**:

SUPINE                         PAST PARTICIPLE

| | | | | |
|---|---|---|---|---|
| bundit → | bund~~it~~ | + en → | bunden | bound |
| försvunnit | försvunn~~it~~ | + en | försvunnen | disappeared |
| skrivit | skriv~~it~~ | + en | skriven | written |
| bjudit | bjud~~it~~ | + en | bjuden | invited |

You can read more about the inflection of participles in 11.8–11.10.

# 9.16 Verbs with two objects

When you learn a new verb, you often have to learn what construction it has; for example, what kind of object can go with the verb. As in English, some verbs can have two objects. An important verb of this type is **ge** 'give'. It can occur in sentences like:

Jag gav paketet till Peter.          I gave the packet to Peter.

**Paketet** 'the packet' is the object in this sentence. But there is another object, **till Peter** 'to Peter'. This second object tells you who received the packet and is preceded by the preposition **till**. There is another construction with the verb **ge**, however, which has an exact parallel in English. You can move the object that is the receiver to a position directly after the verb. The preposition **till** then disappears, as does **to** in English:

Jag gav ~~till~~ Peter paketet.
*i.e.*
Jag gav Peter paketet.          I gave Peter the packet.

There are several verbs in Swedish which have a meaning similar to **ge** 'give'. These verbs can usually be constructed in the same two ways. Some examples of these verbs are:

**skicka (skickar)** 'send'

Vi skickade ett vykort till farmor.
Vi skickade farmor ett vykort.
} We sent grandmother a postcard.

**sända (sänder)** 'send'

Demonstranterna sände ett telegram till statsministern.
Demonstranterna sände statsministern ett telegram.
} The demonstrators sent the prime minister a telegram.

**räcka (räcker)** 'pass'

Peter räckte saxen till Eva.
Peter räckte Eva saxen.
} Peter passed Eva the scissors.

**visa (visar)** 'show'

Vi visade brevet för Olle.
Vi visade Olle brevet.
(N.B. **för**, not **till**)
} We showed Olle the letter.

# 9.17 Verbs with particles

Quite a number of Swedish verbs are followed by particles. Particles are small words that usually have a meaning of their own, for example **upp** 'up', **igen** 'again'. But when they are used together with a verb it is often difficult to recognize this meaning. In many cases you have to learn the verb + particle as one word. This is true, for example, of **känna igen** 'recognize', **slå upp** 'look up' and **tycka om** 'like' in sentences such as:

| | |
|---|---|
| Jag kände igen Lena på fotot. | I recognized Lena in the photo. |
| Jag måste slå upp telefonnumret. | I must look up the phone number. |
| Vi tycker om dig. | We like you. |

The particle, not the verb, is stressed:

| | | |
|---|---|---|
| känna igen | (känner igen) | recognize |
| slå upp | (slår upp) | look up |
| tycka om | (tycker om) | like |

The particle that follows the verb in such verb expressions can easily be mistaken for a preposition. There are quite a few verbs in Swedish that are followed by a special preposition that stands before an object:

| | |
|---|---|
| Sten tittade på TV. | Sten watched TV. |

But this preposition is unstressed, while the verb is stressed:

| | | |
|---|---|---|
| titta på | (tittar på) | look at, watch |

Some prepositions can be used as particles, and are then stressed. This means that certain verbs have completely different meanings when they are followed by, for example, the preposition **på** and the particle **på**:

hälsa på      greet
hälsa på      visit

Jag hälsade på Per.             I greeted Per.
(with the stress on the verb)
Jag hälsade på Per.             I visited Per.
(with the stress on the particle **på**)

Compare the following examples in which **på** and **av** are stressed particles:

sätta på (sätter på):
Jag satte på TV:n.             I put on the TV.

stänga av (stänger av):
Jag stängde av TV:n.           I turned off the TV.

As you will probably have recognized, English uses verbs with particles in a very similar way. But it is important that you learn to stress the Swedish particles in the right way. Listen to your teacher or someone else who can speak Swedish and repeat the sentences in this section.

Note that the particle is normally placed before the object in Swedish, even when the object is a pronoun:

Jag slog upp telefonnumret.      I looked up the phone number.
Jag slog upp det.              I looked it up.

# 10 Forms of the noun

The noun and its forms have already been described briefly in 2.2–2.5. In this chapter we shall be looking at the forms of the noun in greater detail.

## 10.1 *En* words and *ett* words

As we have already seen, Swedish distinguishes between **en** words and **ett** words. In grammatical terms you can say that the noun has two *genders* *(genus)*. Normally you cannot tell whether a word should be an **en** word or an **ett** word. Words with almost identical meanings, for example, can have different genders:

| 'EN' WORDS | | 'ETT' WORDS | |
|---|---|---|---|
| en villa | a house | ett hus | a house, a building |
| en båt | a boat | ett skepp | a ship |

There is one group of nouns that are almost always **en** words. They are nouns that denote people or animals:

| en människa | a person, a human being | en man | a man |
|---|---|---|---|
| en kvinna | a woman | en polis | a policeman |
| en lärare | a teacher | en läkare | a doctor |
| en häst | a horse | en ko | a cow |
| en elefant | an elephant | en fågel | a bird |

Exceptions: **ett barn** 'a child', **ett biträde** 'an assistant', **ett djur** 'an animal'.

Thus, to distinguish between **en** words and **ett** words there is only one rule:

---

Words that denote people and animals are nearly always **en** words.
For other nouns you normally have to learn **en** or **ett** together with the noun.

---

## 10.2 Definiteness

A Swedish noun has an *indefinite (obestämd)* or a *definite (bestämd)* form (compare 2.4).

|  | INDEFINITE FORM | | DEFINITE FORM | |
|---|---|---|---|---|
| *'En' words* | **en** dag | a day | dag**en** | the day |
| *'Ett' words* | **ett** år | a year | år**et** | the year |

The indefinite form is usually marked with an *indefinite article (obestämd artikel)*. This is the same word as the numeral one: **en** or **ett**. The definite form is marked with a *definite article (bestämd artikel)*. The definite article is not a separate word; it is an ending that is added on to the end of the noun. In the examples above it has the form **en** (**dag-en**) or **et** (**år-et**). The definite form is made by adding **en** to an **en** word and **et** to an **ett** word:

---

Definite form:  **en** word + **en**
                  **ett** word + **et**

---

|  | INDEFINITE FORM | |  | | DEFINITE FORM | |
|---|---|---|---|---|---|---|
| *'En' words* | en bil | a car | + en | → | bilen | the car |
|  | en affär | a shop | + en |  | affären | the shop |
|  | en regering | a government | + en |  | regeringen | the government |
| *'Ett' words* | ett brev | a letter | + et | → | brevet | the letter |
|  | ett sätt | a way, manner | + et |  | sättet | the way, manner |
|  | ett beslut | a decision | + et |  | beslutet | the decision |

If the noun ends in a vowel, the definite article loses its **e**, taking the form **n** after **en** words and **t** after **ett** words. The reason is that Swedish always avoids putting two unstressed vowels together:

---

Definite form when the noun ends in a vowel: **en** words + **e̸n**
                                         **ett** words + **e̸t**

---

|  | INDEFINITE FORM | |  | | DEFINITE FORM | |
|---|---|---|---|---|---|---|
| *'En' words* | en villa | a house | + e̸n | → | villan | the house |
|  | en tanke | a thought | + e̸n |  | tanken | the thought |
| *'Ett' words* | ett märke | a mark | + e̸t | → | märket | the mark |
|  | ett hjärta | a heart | + e̸t |  | hjärtat | the heart |

In **en** words which end in unstressed **er** or **el**, the **e** in the definite article disappears:

| INDEFINITE FORM | | DEFINITE FORM | |
|---|---|---|---|
| en åker | a field | + ǝn → åkern | the field |
| en spegel | a mirror | + ǝn → spegeln | the mirror |

In **en** words which end in an unstressed **en**, and in **ett** words which end in unstressed **er, el** or **en**, the unstressed **e** disappears when the definite article is added:

| INDEFINITE FORM | | DEFINITE FORM | |
|---|---|---|---|
| ett undǝr | a miracle | + et → undret | the miracle |
| ett segǝl | a sail | + et → seglet | the sail |
| ett vapǝn | a weapon | + et → vapnet | the weapon |
| en ökǝn | a desert | + en → öknen | the desert |

This is part of a more general rule which says that an unstressed **e** normally disappears in words ending in **er, el** or **en** when an ending beginning with a vowel is added (see also 10.5, 10.8, 11.10 and 14.4).

## 10.3 Use of the definite and indefinite forms

In most cases the use of the definite and the indefinite article in Swedish corresponds to the use of the articles in English. The indefinite form is used when the speaker believes that the noun denotes something unknown to the listener (for example, because it has not been mentioned before). The definite form is used for something that is known to the listener (for example, because it has just been mentioned):

| | |
|---|---|
| Eva är klädd i **en röd kappa** | Eva is dressed in a red coat |
| och **en vit hatt.** | and a white hat. |
| **Kappan** är sliten | The coat is worn out |
| men **hatten** är alldeles ny. | but the hat is quite new. |

There are, however, a few cases where English and Swedish differ. Here are some of them:

**1.** Abstract nouns used in a general sense. Definite article in Swedish:

| | |
|---|---|
| Tid**en** går. | Time flies. |
| Konst**en** är lång, liv**et** är kort. | Art is long, life is short. |
| Ljus**et** går fortare än ljud**et**. | Light travels faster than sound. |

**2.** The definite article in Swedish often corresponds to a possessive in English:

| | |
|---|---|
| Han stoppade hand**en** i fick**an**. | He put his hand in his pocket. |
| Hon tappade balans**en**. | She lost her balance. |
| Jag måste tvätta hår**et**. | I must wash my hair |

**3.** After the verbs **vara** 'be' and **bli** 'become' the indefinite article is omitted before a noun that denotes

*trade or profession:*

| | |
|---|---|
| Eva är lärare. | Eva is a teacher. |
| Lilla Per vill bli polis. | Little Per wants to be a policeman. |

*nationality:*

| | |
|---|---|
| John är engelsman. | John is an Englishman. |

*religious or political affiliation:*

| | |
|---|---|
| Maria blev katolik 1967. | Maria became a Catholic in 1967. |

N.B. If there is an adjective before the noun (see 11.1), the indefinite article is not omitted:

| | |
|---|---|
| Eva är en skicklig lärare. | Eva is a clever teacher. |

## 10.4 Countable and uncountable nouns

Nouns can usually be counted: one car, two cars, three cars etc. Nouns like this are called *countable nouns (räkningsbara substantiv)*. There are, however, other nouns which cannot be counted: meat, iron, gold, sand, milk etc. You cannot say one sand, two sands and so on. These nouns are called *uncountable (icke-räkningsbara)*. They usually denote materials of various kinds. Uncountable nouns cannot have an indefinite article. This is true both in Swedish and in English. But they can take the definite form:

UNCOUNTABLE NOUNS

| INDEFINITE | | DEFINITE | |
|---|---|---|---|
| mjölk | milk | mjölken | the milk |
| kaffe | coffee | kaffet | the coffee |

The word **många** 'many', 'a lot of' followed by the noun in the plural is used to denote a large number of a countable noun.

The word **mycket** 'much', 'a lot of' is used to denote a large quantity of a material which is not countable:

| | |
|---|---|
| Eva rökte **många** cigaretter. | Eva smoked many (a lot of) cigarettes. |
| Eva åt **mycket** mat. | Eva ate a lot of food. |
| Hon drack inte **mycket** vin. | She did not drink much wine. |

## 10.5 The plural forms of nouns

There are five common plural endings in Swedish:

| or | ar | er | n | no ending |
|---|---|---|---|---|
| flick**or** | pojk**ar** | bank**er** | piano**n** | hus (same form as the singular) |
| girls | boys | banks | pianos | houses |

In certain cases you will have to learn what the plural ending of a noun is.

But there are a number of rules that cover many nouns. The choice of ending is decided in the first place by whether the noun is an **en** word or an **ett** word. An **en** word takes one of the endings with an **r** : **or**, **ar** or **er**. Normally an **ett** word takes **n** or no ending in the plural. You can in many cases work out which ending an **en** or an **ett** word should have by looking at the way the noun ends. The most important of these rules are given below. First come the rules for **en** words and then the rules for **ett** words. There are five rules.

**1. En** words that end in an unstressed **a** take the ending **or** in the plural. When you add **or**, the a disappears:

| SINGULAR | | | | PLURAL | |
|---|---|---|---|---|---|
| en klocka | → klocká | + or | → | klockor | watch – watches |
| en skola | skolá | + or | | skolor | school – schools |
| en jacka | jacká | + or | | jackor | coat – coats |
| en soffa | soffá | + or | | soffor | sofa – sofas |
| en skjorta | skjortá | + or | | skjortor | shirt – shirts |

> **En** words that end in **a: or**

**2. En** words that end in an unstressed **e** take the ending **ar** in the plural. When you add **ar**, the e disappears:

| SINGULAR | | | | PLURAL | |
|---|---|---|---|---|---|
| en pojke | → pojké | + ar | → | pojkar | boy – boys |
| en timme | timmé | + ar | | timmar | hour – hours |
| en bulle | bullé | + ar | | bullar | bun – buns |
| en tanke | tanké | + ar | | tankar | thought – thoughts |
| en påse | påsé | + ar | | påsar | bag – bags |

> **En** words that end in **e: ar**

**3. En** words with the stress on the last vowel take **er** in the plural. The word must have more than one vowel (so that the last vowel is not also the first):

| SINGULAR | | | | PLURAL | |
|---|---|---|---|---|---|
| en maskin | → maskin | + er | → | maskiner | machine – machines |
| en cigarett | cigarett | + er | | cigaretter | cigarette – cigarettes |
| en kamrat | kamrat | + er | | kamrater | friend – friends |
| en telefon | telefon | + er | | telefoner | telephone – telephones |
| en industri | industri | + er | | industrier | industry – industries |

> **En** words with the stress on the last vowel: **er**

**4.** **Ett** words that end in a vowel take the ending **n** in the plural:

| SINGULAR | | | | PLURAL | |
|---|---|---|---|---|---|
| ett yrke | → yrke | + n | → | yrken | occupation – occupations |
| ett frimärke | frimärke | + n | | frimärken | stamp – stamps |
| ett rykte | rykte | + n | | rykten | rumour – rumours |
| ett ställe | ställe | + n | | ställen | place – places |
| ett konto | konto | + n | | konton | account – accounts |

> **Ett** words that end in a vowel: **n**

**5.** **Ett** words that end in a consonant take no ending in the plural:

| SINGULAR | PLURAL | |
|---|---|---|
| ett rum | rum | room – rooms |
| ett fönster | fönster | window – windows |
| ett jobb | jobb | job – jobs |
| ett år | år | year – years |
| ett beslut | beslut | decision – decisions |

> **Ett** words that end in a consonant: **no ending**

Unfortunately there are quite a few nouns that are not covered by these five rules. In particular there is no rule for choosing the right plural ending for **en** words that end in a consonant and are not covered by Rule 3. These nouns take either **ar** or **er**:

| SINGULAR | PLURAL | | SINGULAR | PLURAL | |
|---|---|---|---|---|---|
| en bil | bilar | car – cars | en bild | bilder | picture – pictures |
| en buss | bussar | bus – buses | en färg | färger | colour – colours |
| en dag | dagar | day – days | en sak | saker | thing – things |
| en kväll | kvällar | evening – evenings | en gång | gånger | time – times |
| en häst | hästar | horse – horses | en gäst | gäster | guest – guests |

> **En** words that end in a consonant: **ar** or **er**

You will have to learn the plural form of these nouns when you learn the word in the singular. If you want to guess, try **ar**; that is the commonest ending. (But there are many nouns of this type that take **er**, so your guess will often be wrong.)

Note that if the noun ends in unstressed **er**, **el** or **en**, the unstressed **e** disappears before **ar**, **or** and **er**:

| SINGULAR | | | | PLURAL | |
|---|---|---|---|---|---|
| en syster | → | systér | + ar | → systrar | sister – sisters |
| en regel | | regél | + er | → regler | rule – rules |
| en fröken | | frökén | + ar | → fröknar | spinster (Miss) – spinsters |

# 10.6 Plural forms: suffixes

Many nouns are formed with special suffixes, endings that have a particular meaning. All the nouns formed with the same suffix normally have the same gender and the same type of plural ending. There are two very common suffixes in particular that are worth learning right from the start.

**are** (rökare 'smoker')

Many nouns that are formed from a verb and denote a person who does whatever the verb describes end in Swedish in **are**. The English equivalent is **er**. These nouns are always **en** words. Nevertheless they do not have a plural ending:

| SINGULAR | PLURAL | |
|---|---|---|
| en rökare | rökare | smoker – smokers |
| en köpare | köpare | buyer – buyers |
| en väljare | väljare | voter – voters |
| en löntagare | löntagare | wage-earner – wage-earners |
| en ägare | ägare | owner – owners |

**ning** (lösning 'solution')

Many nouns end in **ning**. They are also usually formed from a verb and denote the action itself or its result. Sometimes this ending corresponds to the ending **ing** in English. Nouns ending in **ning** are always **en** words and take **ar** in the plural.

| SINGULAR | | PLURAL | |
|---|---|---|---|
| en övning | + ar | övningar | exercise – exercises |
| en räkning | + ar | räkningar | bill – bills |
| en lösning | + ar | lösningar | solution – solutions |
| en hälsning | + ar | hälsningar | greeting – greetings |
| en landning | + ar | landningar | landing – landings |

## 10.7 Nouns that change their vowel in the plural

There is one group of nouns that change their vowel in the plural. Usually they take the ending **er**. Only certain types of vowel change occur and they are listed below. There are not many nouns of this type, but most of them are quite common. So it is worth learning the forms early.

| SINGULAR | PLURAL | SINGULAR | PLURAL |
|---|---|---|---|
| **a** | **ä** | **o** | **ö** |
| en natt | nätter | en bonde | bönder |
| a night | nights | a farmer | farmers |
| en stad | städer | en ledamot | ledamöter |
| a town | towns | a member | members |
| en hand | händer | | |
| a hand | hands | *A few common nouns of this type* | |
| en tand | tänder | *double the consonant in the* | |
| a tooth | teeth | *plural and make the vowel short:* | |
| en strand | stränder | en fot | fötter |
| a beach | beaches | a foot | feet |
| en rand | ränder | en rot | rötter |
| a stripe | stripes | a root | roots |
| ett land | länder | en bok | böcker |
| a country | countries | a book | books |

Note the following common noun which is completely irregular:

| SINGULAR INDEFINITE | SINGULAR DEFINITE | PLURAL INDEFINITE | PLURAL DEFINITE |
|---|---|---|---|
| en man | mannen | män | männen |
| a man | the man | men | the men |

Note also the word **människa** 'person', 'human being', which has the plural form **människor** 'people'. The **sk** in this word is pronounced *sh*.

## 10.8 The definite form in the plural

When a noun is in the plural, the definite article has a different form from the singular. There are three different forms of the definite article in the plural: **na**, **en** and **a**. The first form, **na**, is used when the noun has a plural form ending in **r** (= the plural endings **or, ar** and **er**):

| INDEFINITE PLURAL | | | DEFINITE PLURAL | |
|---|---|---|---|---|
| klockor | + na | → | klockorna | watches – the watches |
| skolor | + na | | skolorna | schools – the schools |
| pojkar | + na | | pojkarna | boys – the boys |
| timmar | + na | | timmarna | hours – the hours |
| cigaretter | + na | | cigaretterna | cigarettes – the cigarettes |
| maskiner | + na | | maskinerna | machines – the machines |

The other two forms of the definite article go with **ett** words in the plural. **Ett** words that end in a vowel in the singular and take **n** in the plural have the definite form **a** in the plural:

| INDEFINITE PLURAL | | | DEFINITE PLURAL | |
|---|---|---|---|---|
| äpplen | + a | → | äpplena | apples – the apples |
| yrken | + a | | yrkena | occupations – the occupations |
| frimärken | + a | | frimärkena | stamps – the stamps |
| konton | + a | | kontona | accounts – the accounts |

**Ett** words which end in a consonant in the singular and have no ending in the plural have the definite form **en** in the plural:

| INDEFINITE PLURAL | | | DEFINITE PLURAL | |
|---|---|---|---|---|
| jobb | + en | → | jobben | jobs – the jobs |
| beslut | + en | | besluten | decisions – the decisions |
| år | + en | | åren | years – the years |

Note that if the noun ends in unstressed **er**, **el** or **en**, the unstressed **e** disappears when **en** is added:

| INDEFINITE PLURAL | | | DEFINITE PLURAL | |
|---|---|---|---|---|
| mönst∉r | + en | → | mönstren | patterns – the patterns |
| seg∉l | + en | | seglen | sails – the sails |
| teck∉n | + en | | tecknen | signs – the signs |

With a noun which ends in **are**, the definite article has the form **na** in the plural, and the **e** disappears:

| INDEFINITE PLURAL | | | DEFINITE PLURAL | |
|---|---|---|---|---|
| rökar∉ | + na | → | rökarna | smokers – the smokers |

## 10.9 Plurals: summary

The most important rules for the noun in the plural are summarized in the table below. It shows the formation of both the indefinite and the definite forms in the plural.

| | SINGULAR | | PLURAL INDEFINITE | | DEFINITE |
|---|---|---|---|---|---|
| *'En' words* | | | | | |
| ending in **a** | en gata gatá | **or** | | | gator |
| | a street | | | **na** | gatorna |
| ending in **e** | en timme timmé | **ar** | | | timmar |
| | an hour | | | **na** | timmarna |
| with the stress | en cigarett | **er** | | | cigaretter |
| on the last | a cigarette | | | **na** | cigaretterna |
| vowel | | | | | |
| *'Ett' words* | | | | | |
| ending in | ett möte | **n** | | | möten |
| a vowel | a meeting | | | **a** | mötena |
| ending in a | ett glas | **–** | | | glas |
| consonant | a glass | | | **en** | glasen |

## 10.10 The genitive

Swedish nouns have only one case ending, the *genitive (genitiv)*. The genitive denotes a person or thing that possesses something, in the widest sense of the word 'possess'.

| | |
|---|---|
| Olles dotter är 12 år. | Olle's daughter is 12 years old. |
| Sveriges huvudstad heter Stockholm. | The capital of Sweden is Stockholm. |

The genitive is easily formed. You just add an s to the end of the word. If the noun already has an ending, add s to the ending.

| | | | |
|---|---|---|---|
| Olle | + s | Olles syster är sjuk. | Olle's sister is ill. |
| Pojken | + s | Pojkens cykel är trasig. | The boy's bike is broken. |
| Pojkarna | + s | Pojkarnas lärare blev arg. | The boys' teacher was angry. |
| Gatorna | + s | Gatornas namn står på kartan. | The street names are on the map. |

As you can see from the above examples, the genitive in Swedish has a wider use than the 's genitive in English, but in most cases usage is the same.

Note, however, that the genitive s in Swedish does not need an apostrophe.

# 11 Adjectival agreement

## 11.1 The adjective and the noun phrase

This chapter deals with adjectives and other words that qualify or describe nouns. Most adjectives can be both attributive and predicative. Adjectives are *attributive (attributiva)* when they premodify nouns, i.e. when they appear between the determiner (e.g. 'the', 'this') and its noun:

| Determiner | Adjective | Noun |
|------------|-----------|------|
| The        | –         | girl |
| The        | little    | girl |
| This       | little    | girl |

This word group, consisting of determiner + adjective + noun, is called a *noun phrase (NP)*, and the noun is called the *head (huvudord)*. The NP can function as the subject, object or *complement (predikatsfyllnad)* of a sentence and as complement in prepositional phrases:

>          NP                    NP
> The young man kissed his pretty girlfriend.
>     subject                object

>          NP                        NP
> The Iron Maiden was a medieval instrument of torture.
>     subject                complement

>                         NP
>     NP              NP              NP
> The angry man in the front row hurled rotten eggs.
>                 prep. phrase       object
>     subject

Predicative adjectives are adjectives that appear after the verb:

>          NP
> Two thousand men were made redundant.
>     subject       verb  adjective

Predicative adjectives can define the subject:

The pupil is **clever.**
The children are getting **tired.**
The discussion became **heated.**

They may also define the object:

> The Depression left him **penniless.**
> You make me very **unhappy.**
> Elaine found the concert **boring.**

In English, adjectives, whether attributive or predicative, do not change their form. In Swedish, however, all nouns, both attributive and predicative, change their form according to the gender and number of the noun they qualify. This is called *adjectival agreement (kongruens).* Here are some examples:

| | |
|---|---|
| Den här bilen är **röd.** | This car is red. |
| De här bilarna är **röda.** | These cars are red. |
| Det här huset är **rött.** | This house is red. |
| De här husen är **röda.** | These houses are red. |

The forms of the adjectives will be explained in detail in the following sections.

Adjectives can also function as the heads of noun phrases, both in Swedish and in English. This construction is, however, much more common in Swedish than it is in English, where it is restricted to categories of people. In most other cases English uses a pronoun or noun as a 'prop', e.g. 'one(s)', 'thing', 'man', 'woman', etc.

| | |
|---|---|
| **de sjuka** | the sick |
| **de fattiga** | the poor |
| **det okända** | the unknown |
| **den gamle** | the old man |
| **de avskedade** | the dismissed workers |
| **det väsentliga** | the vital thing |

| | |
|---|---|
| Han märkte inte **det löjliga** i situationen. | He failed to see the ridiculous side of the situation. |
| **Det värsta** med honom är att han inte tål kritik. | The worst thing about him is that he can't stand criticism. |

# 11.2 Articles and adjectives in the indefinite form

An adjective may premodify a noun. If the noun is an **en** word in the indefinite form, the adjective does not change.

| INDEFINITE ARTICLE | ADJECTIVE | NOUN | |
|---|---|---|---|
| **en** | grön | stol | a green chair |
| **en** | hög | mur | a high wall |
| **en** | dyr | klocka | an expensive watch |
| | kall | mjölk | cold milk (uncountable) |

The adjective takes the ending **t** if the noun is an **ett** word. Note that this also applies to adjectives that premodify uncountable nouns.

| INDEFINITE ARTICLE | ADJECTIVE | NOUN | |
|---|---|---|---|
| **ett** | grönt | bord | a green table |
| **ett** | högt | hus | a tall building |
| **ett** | dyrt | hotell | an expensive hotel |
| | kallt | kaffe | cold coffee (uncountable) |

Below you can see some sentences in which the adjective and the noun together act as a noun phrase:

| | |
|---|---|
| Jag kan se **en hög mur.** | I can see a high wall. |
| Jag kan se **ett högt hus** i parken. | I can see a tall building in the park. |
| **En dyr klocka** bör gå rätt. | An expensive watch should keep time. |
| **Ett dyrt hotell** bör ha god service. | An expensive hotel should have good service. |

# 11.3 Articles and adjectives in the definite form

If you premodify a noun in the definite form with an adjective, there are several effects: the adjective takes a special ending, **a**; also, a special definite article is placed in front of the adjective. This article has the form **den** in front of **en** words and **det** in front of **ett** words (in the singular). In addition, there is the usual definite ending to the noun:

| | DEFINITE ARTICLE | ADJECTIVE | NOUN | |
|---|---|---|---|---|
| | **den** | gröna | stolen | the green chair |
| *'En'* | **den** | höga | muren | the high wall |
| *words* | **den** | dyra | klockan | the expensive watch |
| | **den** | kalla | mjölken | the cold milk |
| | **det** | gröna | bordet | the green table |
| *'Ett'* | **det** | höga | huset | the tall building |
| *words* | **det** | dyra | hotellet | the expensive hotel |
| | **det** | kalla | kaffet | the cold coffee |

Here are a few examples of the changes that take place between the indefinite and the definite forms:

| | |
|---|---|
| Jag kan se **en hög mur** och **ett högt hus.** | I can see a high wall and a tall building. |
| **Den höga muren** döljer nästan helt **det höga huset.** | The high wall almost completely conceals the tall building. |

| Peter köpte **en dyr klocka** och **en billig klocka.** **Den dyra klockan** har stannat, men **den billiga klockan** går fortfarande. | Peter bought an expensive watch and a cheap watch. The expensive watch has stopped, but the cheap watch is still going. |
| --- | --- |

## 11.4 Articles and adjectives in the plural

When the noun is in the plural, the adjective always takes the ending **a**. If the noun is indefinite, you do not need a special article. Often, however, the word **några** 'some' is used. Note that there is no difference in the adjective forms between **en** words and **ett** words in the plural:

| (INDEFINITE ARTICLE) | ADJECTIVE | NOUN | |
| --- | --- | --- | --- |
| *'En'* (några) | gröna | stolar | (some) green chairs |
| *words* (några) | höga | murar | (some) high walls |
| *'Ett'* (några) | gröna | bord | (some) green tables |
| *words* (några) | höga | hus | (some) tall buildings |

If the noun has the definite form in the plural, an article must be placed in front of the noun if there is also an attributive adjective. In the plural this article has the form **de** for both **en** and **ett** words:

| DEFINITE ARTICLE | ADJECTIVE | NOUN | |
| --- | --- | --- | --- |
| *'En* **de** | gröna | stol**arna** | the green chairs |
| *words* **de** | höga | mur**arna** | the high walls |
| *'Ett'* **de** | gröna | bor**den** | the green tables |
| *words* **de** | höga | hus**en** | the tall buildings |

Here are a few examples of indefinite and definite noun phrases in the plural:

| Vi sålde **några bruna stolar** och **några röda bord.** **De bruna stolarna** passade inte till **de röda borden.** Fängelset har **höga murar. De höga murarna** gör det svårt att rymma. | We sold some brown chairs and some red tables. The brown chairs did not match the red tables. The prison has high walls. The high walls make it difficult to escape. |
| --- | --- |

We have now dealt with all the forms of the definite article placed before an attributive adjective. They can be summarized in the following table:

| SINGULAR | | PLURAL |
|---|---|---|
| **En** words: **den** | **Ett** words: **det** | **de** |
| **den** dyra klockan | **det** dyra hotellet | **de** dyra klockorna |

There is no article before the noun if the defined noun has no attributive adjective. Compare these examples:

| | |
|---|---|
| Kan du se **det höga huset?** | Can you see the tall building? |
| Kan du se **huset?** | Can you see the building? |
| Eva sitter på **den gröna stolen.** | Eva is sitting on the green chair. |
| Eva sitter på **stolen.** | Eva is sitting on the chair. |
| Banken äger **de dyra hotellen.** | The bank owns the expensive hotels. |
| Banken äger **hotellen.** | The bank owns the hotels. |

## 11.5 Predicative adjectives

When an adjective is in a predicative position, it agrees with the noun which is the subject. The forms of the adjective are the same here as when the adjective is used attributively in an indefinite noun phrase. Adjectives are used predicatively after verbs like **vara** 'be', **bli** 'become', 'get', and **göra** 'make':

| | SUBJECT | VERB | COMPLEMENT | |
|---|---|---|---|---|
| SINGULAR | Filmen | är | rolig. | The film is amusing. |
| *'En' words* | Maten | blev | kall. | The food got cold. |
| | Han | gjorde | henne lycklig. | He made her happy. |
| *'Ett' words* | Programmet | är | roligt. | The programme is amusing. |
| +t | Vädret | blev | kallt. | The weather got cold. |
| | Vi | målade | huset rött. | We painted the house red. |
| PLURAL | Filmerna | är | roliga. | The films are amusing. |
| +a | Elementen | blev | kalla. | The radiators got cold. |
| | De | kallade | oss dumma. | They called us stupid. |

## 11.6 Summary of the forms of the adjective

We have now dealt with all the forms of the adjective. They are summarized in the following table:

| | FORMS OF THE ADJECTIVE | |
|---|---|---|
| | INDEFINITE SINGULAR AND PREDICATIVE | DEFINITE AND PLURAL |
| **En** words | **grön**<br>en **grön** stol<br>Stolen är **grön**. | **grön + a → gröna**<br>den gröna stolen<br>det gröna bordet |
| **Ett** words | **grön + t → grönt**<br>ett grönt bord<br>Bordet är grönt. → | (några) gröna stolar<br>(några) gröna bord<br>Stolarna är gröna.<br>Borden är gröna. |

## 11.7 The adjective *liten*

The adjective **liten** 'little', 'small' changes its form in a different way from other adjectives. In the plural the word is replaced by another word, **små**.

| | PREDICATIVE | INDEFINITE FORM | DEFINITE FORM |
|---|---|---|---|
| SINGULAR | Skjortan är **liten**.<br>The shirt is small. | en **liten** skjorta<br>a small shirt | den **lilla** skjortan<br>the small shirt |
| | Skåpet är **litet**.<br>The cupboard is small. | ett **litet** skåp<br>a small cupboard | det **lilla** skåpet<br>the small cupboard |
| PLURAL | Skjortorna är **små**.<br>The shirts are small. | två **små** skjortor<br>two small shirts | de **små** skåpen<br>the small cupboards |

## 11.8 Agreement of the participles

As we saw in 9.13 the participle forms of the verb may function as adjectives. The past participle (9.15) agrees with its noun in the same way as an adjective by adding **t** and **a**:

| | PREDICATIVE | INDEFINITE FORM | DEFINITE FORM |
|---|---|---|---|
| SINGULAR | Dörren är stängd.<br>The door is closed. | en stängd dörr<br>a closed door | den stängda dörren<br>the closed door |
| | Fönstret är stängt.<br>The window is closed. | ett stängt fönster<br>a closed window | det stängda fönstret<br>the closed window |
| PLURAL | Dörrarna är stängda.<br>The doors are closed. | två stängda dörrar<br>two closed doors | de stängda dörrarna<br>the closed doors |

The present participle, which ends in **ande** or **ende**, does not change its form:

| | |
|---|---|
| Informationen var uppmuntrande. | The information was encouraging. |
| Meddelandet var uppmuntrande. | The message was encouraging. |
| ett uppmuntrande meddelande | an encouraging message |
| det uppmuntrande meddelandet | the encouraging message |

## 11.9 The *t* form of the past participle and of certain adjectives

When the ending **t** is added to a past participle or an adjective that already ends in a **t** or a **d**, a complication arises. The basic rule is:

> **t** and **d** disappear in front of the ending **t**.

| | | | | | |
|---|---|---|---|---|---|
| svart | → | svar~~t~~ | + t → | svart | black |
| låst | | lås~~t~~ | + t | låst | locked |
| hård | | hår~~d~~ | + t | hårt | hard |
| stängd | | stäng~~d~~ | + t | stängt | closed |
| öppnad | | öppna~~d~~ | + t | öppnat | opened |

| | |
|---|---|
| en **svart** dörr | a black door |
| ett **svart** skåp | a black cupboard |
| en **hård** bulle | a hard bun |
| ett **hårt** käx | a hard biscuit |
| en **öppnad** burk | an opened tin |
| ett **öppnat** brev | an opened letter |

There are certain types of past participle and adjective that take the ending **tt** instead of **t**. The first type comprises past participles that end in **dd**:

> Past participles that end in **dd** change **dd** into **tt**.

| | | | | | |
|---|---|---|---|---|---|
| klädd | | klä~~dd~~ | + tt → | klätt | dressed |
| försedd | | förse~~dd~~ | + tt | försett | equipped |

| | |
|---|---|
| Bilen är **försedd** med dimljus. | The car is equipped with fog lights. |
| Köket är **försett** med fläkt. | The kitchen is equipped with a fan. |

The second type comprises adjectives that end in a long stressed vowel, sometimes followed by a **d** or a **t**. These adjectives also take **tt**. If there was originally a **t** or a **d** at the end, this disappears and the vowel becomes short:

The adjective ends in

| | | | | | | |
|---|---|---|---|---|---|---|
| a long stressed vowel | blå | | + tt | → | blått | blue |
| | ny | | + tt | | nytt | new |
| a long stressed vowel + t | vit | vit | + tt | → | vitt | white |
| | söt | söt | + tt | | sött | sweet |
| a long stressed vowel + d | röd | röd | + tt | → | rött | red |
| | bred | bred | + tt | | brett | broad |

Note the short vowel before **tt**.

| | |
|---|---|
| en **ny** skjorta | a new shirt |
| ett **nytt** skärp | a new belt |
| Flickan är **söt**. | The girl is pretty. |
| Barnet är **sött**. | The child is pretty. |
| en **bred** gata | a broad street |
| ett **brett** leende | a broad smile |

Adjectives and past participles that end in unstressed **en** (an unstressed **e** followed by **n**) lose the **n** when **t** is added:

---

Adjectives and past participles: e**n** + t → **et**

---

| | | | | | |
|---|---|---|---|---|---|
| öppen | → | öppen | + t | → öppet | open |
| naken | | naken | + t | naket | naked |
| skriven | | skriven | + t | skrivet | written |
| försvunnen | | försvunnen | + t | försvunnet | disappeared |

| | |
|---|---|
| en **naken** pojke | a naked boy |
| ett **naket** barn | a naked child |
| Romanen är **skriven** på engelska. | The novel is written in English. |
| Brevet är **skrivet** med bläck. | The letter is written in ink. |

Note that if the vowel **e** is stressed, the **n** does not disappear: ren + t → rent 'clean'.

# 11.10 The inflection of certain participles and adjectives

A past participle formed from an **ar** verb ends in **ad**. These participles take an **e** instead of an **a** in the plural and before nouns in the definite form:

---

Past participles that end in **ad** take **e** instead of **a**.

---

| | | |
|---|---|---|
| öppnad + e | → öppnade | opened |
| målad + e | målade | painted |
| Compare: | | |
| stängd + a | stängda | closed |

|  |  |
|---|---|
| | Compare: |
| Dörren är öppnad. | Dörren är stängd. |
| The door is opened. | The door is closed. |
| Dörrarna är öppnade. | Dörrarna är stängda. |
| The doors are opened. | The doors are closed. |
| de öppnade dörrarna | de stängda dörrarna |
| the opened doors | the closed doors |
| en nymålad stol | en nyköpt stol |
| a newly painted chair | a newly bought chair |
| två nymålade stolar | två nyköpta stolar |
| two newly painted chairs | two newly bought chairs |

The next rule is common to participles and adjectives:

---

Past participles and adjectives that end in unstressed **er, el** or **en** lose the **e** when **a** is added.

---

| | | | |
|---|---|---|---|
| skriven | → skriv⁄en + a | → skrivna | written |
| bunden | bund⁄en + a | bundna | bound |
| naken | nak⁄en + a | nakna | naked |
| enkel | enk⁄el + a | enkla | simple |
| säker | säk⁄er + a | säkra | sure |

In a few adjectives another vowel disappears:

| | | | |
|---|---|---|---|
| gammal | gamm⁄al + a | | gamla (see 8.16.) old |

The vowel only disappears if it is unstressed:

| | | | |
|---|---|---|---|
| ren + a | → rena | clean | |
| hel + a | hela | whole | |

# 12 Possessive pronouns and the genitive

## 12.1 Possessive pronouns

Personal pronouns have special forms to denote an owner, or someone who possesses something in the widest sense of the word. These forms are called *possessive pronouns (possessiva pronomen)*. They are the forms of the personal pronoun that correspond to the genitive of the noun (10.10).

| | |
|---|---|
| **Min** bror bor i London. | My brother lives in London. |
| **Din** syster är söt. | Your sister is pretty. |
| Känner du Per? **Hans** mor är | Do you know Per? His mother |
| **vår** svensklärare. | is our Swedish teacher. |
| **Hennes** man är **er** nya lärare. | Her husband is your new teacher. |
| Känner du familjen Persson? | Do you know the Perssons? |
| **Deras** villa är till salu. | Their house is for sale. |

There is also a special possessive form of **den** and **det**, which is **dess**. But for various reasons **dess** is not used very much. The idea is usually expressed in a different way:

| | |
|---|---|
| Jag kan se en katt. | I can see a cat. |
| **Dess** päls är grå. | Its coat is grey. |
| Preferably: | |
| Den har grå päls. | It has a grey coat. |

## 12.2 The reflexive form of the possessive pronoun: *sin*

When the third person possessive pronoun refers to the subject of the same clause, **sin** is used. Thus **sin** may mean 'his', 'her', 'its' or 'their'. If you cannot insert 'own' after the pronoun in English, you must use **hans, hennes, dess, deras**. The word **sin** is the possessive counterpart of the object form **sig** (5.2).

SUBJECT

**Per** besöker **sin** mamma ofta.
Per often visits his mother.

Eva är gift med **Per.**
Eva is married to Per.

Hon ringer **hans** mamma varje dag.
She phones his mother every day.

**Eva** tvättar inte **sin** bil.
Eva does not wash her (own) car.

100

| | |
|---|---|
| Per gillar **Eva**, så | han tvättar **hennes** bil. |
| Per likes Eva, so | he washes her car. |
| Jag kan se en katt. | **Den** slickar **sin** päls. |
| I can see a cat. | It is licking its coat. |
| | **Per och Eva** reparerade **sin** villa. |
| | Per and Eva repaired their house. |
| Nu har **de** flyttat, så | vi har köpt **deras** villa. |
| Now they have moved, so | we have bought their house. |

Note that **sin** cannot be used with the subject:

| | |
|---|---|
| Jag känner **Per**. | I know Per. |
| **Hans** (*not* sin) bror arbetar på vårt kontor. | His brother works at our office. |

The following table shows the possessive forms of all the personal pronouns:

| SUBJECT | NON-REFLEXIVE | REFLEXIVE |
|---|---|---|
| jag | min | min |
| du | din | din |
| han | hans | **sin** |
| hon | hennes | **sin** |
| den | (dess) | **sin** |
| det | (dess) | **sin** |
| vi | vår | vår |
| ni | er | er |
| de | deras | **sin** |

## 12.3 The forms of the possessive pronouns

Some of the possessive pronouns have forms that are similar to those of the adjective when it is used attributively. They take a **t** when they come before an **ett** word in the singular and an **a** before a noun in the plural:

| | |
|---|---|
| Kan du se **vår** bil? (**en** word in the singular) | Can you see our car? |
| Kan du se **vårt** hus? (**ett** word) | Can you see our house? |
| Kan du se **våra** bilar? (plural) | Can you see our cars? |

101

Others, however, have irregular forms and several do not change their form at all. The following table shows all the forms:

| SINGULAR | | PLURAL |
|---|---|---|
| *'En' words* | *'Ett' words* | |
| **min** bil | **mitt** hus | **mina** bilar |
| **din** bil | **ditt** hus | **dina** bilar |
| **sin** bil | **sitt** hus | **sina** bilar |
| **hans** bil | **hans** hus | **hans** bilar |
| **hennes** bil | **hennes** hus | **hennes** bilar |
| **dess** bil | **dess** hus | **dess** bilar |
| **vår** bil | **vårt** hus | **våra** bilar |
| **er** bil | **ert** hus | **era** bilar |
| **deras** bil | **deras** hus | **deras** bilar |

The basic rule is: add **t** before an **ett** word and **a** before a plural.

The irregular forms follow two rules:

1. Words ending in **s** do not change their forms: **hans, hennes, dess, deras.**
2. The rhyming words **min, din, sin** change **n** to **tt** before **ett** words: **mitt, ditt, sitt.**

There are no special forms in Swedish for the possessive pronouns used as predicatives, such as the English 'mine', 'yours', etc. Exactly the same forms as above are used:

| | |
|---|---|
| Det här är min bil. | This is my car. |
| Den är **min.** | It is mine. |
| Ert hus är större än **vårt.** | Your house is larger than ours. |
| Det är inte **hennes**, det är **deras.** | It isn't hers, it's theirs. |

Another difference between the use of the possessive pronouns in Swedish and English is that with parts of the body, clothing and other things which are personal belongings, Swedish uses the definite article, not the possessive pronoun.

| | |
|---|---|
| Han hade handen i fickan. | He had his hand in his pocket. |
| Har du bilen med dig? | Have you got your car with you? |
| Hon ryckte på axlarna. | She shrugged her shoulders. |

## 12.4 The forms of nouns and adjectives after the genitive and possessives

It is important to notice how the possessive pronouns affect the form of the other words in a noun phrase. The noun which has the possessive pronoun as modifier does not take a final definite article:

| min bil | *Wrong:* | min bilen |
| hans hus | *Wrong:* | hans huset |

The same is true of nouns that follow the s genitive (10.10):

| Olles bil | *Wrong:* | Olles bilen |

Note, too, that the adjective always takes the ending **a** after a genitive or a possessive:

| mitt grön**a** bord | my green table |
| Olles röd**a** bil | Olle's red car |

Note the following rules:

---

After a possessive pronoun or a noun in the genitive:
- no article or definite form of the noun
- always the ending **a** on the adjective

---

# 13 Some more determiners

## 13.1 *den här* and *den där*

'This' and 'that' are two very common determiners in English. They correspond in Swedish to **den här** 'this' and **den där** 'that'. These expressions consist of the definite article followed by the word **här** 'here' and **där** 'there'. The definite article agrees in the usual way with the noun. The forms are given in the following table:

|  | SINGULAR | | PLURAL |
|--|----------|--|--------|
|  | *'En' words* | *'Ett' words* | |
| 'this' | **den här** biljetten<br>this ticket | **det här** tåget<br>this train | **de här** biljetterna<br>these tickets |
| 'that' | **den här** biljetten<br>that ticket | **det där** tåget<br>that train | **de där** tågen<br>those trains |

Note, too, what happens to the noun and the adjectives after **den här** and **den där**:

| | |
|--|--|
| den här dyra biljetten | this expensive ticket |
| det där röda tåget | that red train |
| de där dyra biljetterna | those expensive tickets |
| de här röda tågen | these red trains |

---

The noun is always in the definite form after **den här** and **den där**. Adjectives take the ending **a** when they come after **den här** and **den där**.

---

Here are some examples of this type of noun phrase in complete sentences:

| | |
|--|--|
| Vi ska åka med det där röda tåget. | We're going on that red train. |
| Den här biljetten var väldigt dyr. | This ticket was terribly expensive. |
| Per brukar sitta på den här<br>gröna stolen. | Per usually sits on this<br>green chair. |
| Jag föredrar det där dyra hotellet. | I prefer that expensive hotel. |
| De där vita husen är vackra. | Those white houses are beautiful. |

**Den här** and **den där** can also be used predicatively, that is, when the noun is understood. **Den här** and **den där** change their form according to the noun that is understood:

| | |
|---|---|
| Har du en korkskruv? | Have you got a corkscrew? |
| Ja, ta **den här**. | Yes, take this one. |
| Har du ett suddgummi? | Have you got a rubber? |
| Ja, ta **det här**. | Yes, take this one. |
| Har du några handskar? | Have you got any gloves? |
| Nej, får jag låna **de här**? | No, may I borrow these? |

Note that Swedish has no word corresponding to 'one'.

## 13.2 *vilken*

The question word **vilken** corresponds to both 'which' and 'what' before a noun in English. It differs from the question words we have already dealt with in 4.4 because it agrees with the following noun. The forms are as follows:

SINGULAR

PLURAL

*'En' words*

*'Ett' words*

**Vilken** månad är du född?
Which month were you born in?

**Vilket** år är du född?
Which year were you born?

**Vilka** dagar arbetar du?
Which days do you work?

**Vilken** lärare har ni?
Which teacher do you have?

**Vilket** barn är ditt?
Which child is yours?

**Vilka** elever är sjuka idag?
Which pupils are ill today?

**Vilken** dag är det idag?
What day is it today?

**Vilket** pris fick du betala?
What price did you have to pay?

**Vilka** metoder använder de?
What methods do they use?

**Vilken** must be used as the equivalent of 'which' and 'what' when the question word is combined with a noun to form a noun phrase. **Vad** cannot be used together with a noun, as 'what' can in English. **Vilken** can also stand by itself, as in the following examples, where it corresponds to the English 'which one'. As in English, the question indicates some sort of choice. Compare:

| | |
|---|---|
| **Vad** vill du ha? | What would you like? |
| Här är fem apelsiner. | Here are five oranges. |
| **Vilken** vill du ha? | Which one would you like? |
| Här är fem äpplen. | Here are five apples. |
| **Vilket** vill du ha? | Which one would you like? |
| Du får ta två äpplen. | You can take two apples. |
| **Vilka** vill du ha? | Which ones would you like? |
| **Vilket** är det bästa märket? | Which is the best brand? |

**Vilken** is also used in exclamations together with a noun, and corresponds to the English 'What (a)!':

| | |
|---|---|
| **Vilken** underbar utsikt! | What a wonderful view! |
| **Vilket** förfärligt väder! | What terrible weather! |

Note that the indefinite article is not used after **vilken**.

If there is no noun, the following construction is used:

| | |
|---|---|
| Vad rädd jag blev! | How frightened I was! |
| Vad söt du är! | How pretty you are! |

Note the word order; it is the same in Swedish and English.

## 13.3 *någon*

**Någon** corresponds to both 'some' and 'any' in English. It has the following forms:

| SINGULAR | | PLURAL |
|---|---|---|
| *'En' words* | *'Ett' words* | |
| **någon** bok | **något** träd | **några** stolar |
| some (any) book | some (any) tree | some (any) chairs |
| | **någonting** | |
| | something (anything) | |

**Någon (något, några) (nån, nåt, nåra**, in spoken Swedish) can be used both attributively (before a noun), and by itself (without a following noun):

| | |
|---|---|
| Eva bor i **någon** by på landet. | Eva lives in some village in the country. |
| Finns det **någon** tid kvar? | Is there any time left? |
| Hästen hade **något** konstigt märke på halsen. | The horse had some strange mark on its neck. |
| Vi köpte inte **något** vin. | We didn't buy any wine. |
| **Några** av mina vänner var där. | Some of my friends were there. |
| Jag kan inte se **några** böcker. | I can't see any books. |
| Jag behöver en skruvmejsel. Har du **någon**? | I need a screwdriver. Have you got one? |
| Jag vill ha lite vin. Har du **något** kvar? | I'd like some wine. Have you got any left? |
| Mina cigaretter har tagit slut. Har du **några** att ge mig? | I've run out of cigarettes. Have you got any you can give me? |

When **någon** is used by itself, it also corresponds to 'someone' ('somebody'), and 'anyone' ('anybody'):

| | |
|---|---|
| **Någon** har varit här. | Someone has been here. |
| Har **någon** ringt? | Has anyone rung? |

When **något** is used by itself, it also corresponds to 'something' and 'anything'. An alternative to **något** in this use is **någonting**, which is really **någon** + **ting** 'thing', to mean 'something or other'.

| | |
|---|---|
| **Något (Någonting)** måste ha hänt. | Something must have happened. |
| Kan du se **något (någonting)?** | Can you see anything? |

**Någonstans** corresponds to 'somewhere', 'anywhere':

| | |
|---|---|
| Han bor **någonstans** här. | He lives somewhere here. |
| Har du **någonstans** att bo? | Have you got anywhere to live? |

**Någon gång** corresponds to 'some time', 'ever':

| | |
|---|---|
| **någon gång** i framtiden | some time in the future |
| Har du varit där **någon gång?** | Have you ever been there? |

Note that **någon** and **något** are often used to correspond to 'a' and 'an' in yes/no questions, negated clauses (with **inte**) and conditional clauses (introduced by **om** 'if'):

| | |
|---|---|
| Har du **någon** cykel? | Have you got a bike? |
| Jag har inte **något** paraply. | I haven't got an umbrella. |
| Om du ser **någon** azalea i blomsteraffären kan du väl köpa en åt mig. | If you see an azalea in the flower shop you can buy one for me, can't you? |

## 13.4 *inte någon – ingen*

You can add the negative **inte** 'not' to a sentence that contains **någon**. However, you can sometimes replace **inte någon** with **ingen**, just as in English you can replace 'not any' with 'no'.

| | |
|---|---|
| Vi har inte någon mjölk.<br>We don't have any milk. | = Vi har ingen mjölk.<br>We have no milk. |

**Ingen** has the following forms:

| SINGULAR | | PLURAL |
|---|---|---|
| *'En' words* | *'Ett' words* | |
| **ingen** bok<br>no book | **inget** träd<br>no tree | **inga** stolar<br>no chairs |
| | **ingenting**<br>nothing | |

Compare the following examples:

| | |
|---|---|
| Jag har inte någon svart kostym.<br>I haven't got a black suit. | = Jag har ingen svart kostym.<br>I have no black suit. |
| Jag har inte något paraply.<br>I haven't got an umbrella. | = Jag har inget paraply.<br>I have no umbrella. |
| Jag har inte några handskar.<br>I haven't got any gloves. | = Jag har inga handskar.<br>I have no gloves. |
| Jag såg inte någon ute på gatan.<br>I didn't see anyone in the street. | = Jag såg ingen ute på gatan.<br>I saw no one in the street. |
| Jag köpte inte något (inte någonting) i affären.<br>I didn't buy anything in the shop. | = Jag köpte inget (ingenting) i affären.<br>I bought nothing in the shop. |

107

**Ingen** can only be used instead of **inte någon** when the words **inte** and **någon** stand together. This means that you cannot use **ingen** in subordinate clauses or in main clauses with more than one verb. Compare the following examples:

| *Main clause* | *Subordinate clause* |
|---|---|
| Vi har **inte något** salt. | Vi måste låna, om vi **inte** har |
| = Vi har **inget** salt. | **något** salt. |
| We haven't got any salt. | We shall have to borrow some, if we haven't |
| = We have no salt. | got any salt. |
| Hade du **inte några** pengar? | Varför tror du, att jag **inte** hade |
| = Hade du **inga** pengar? | **några** pengar? |
| Didn't you have any money? | Why do you think that I didn't have |
| = Had you no money? | any money? |

| *Main clause, one verb* | *Main clause, more than one verb* |
|---|---|
| Vi har **inte någon** lök. | Jag har **inte** köpt **någon** lök. |
| = Vi har **ingen** lök. | I haven't bought any onions. |
| We haven't got any onions. | |
| = We have no onions. | |

When the negated phrase acts as the subject, **ingen (inget, inga)** is usually preferred as an alternative to **inte någon (något, några)**:

| (**Inte någon** har ätit upp maten.) | = **Ingen** har ätit upp maten. |
|---|---|
| | No one has eaten up their food. |
| (**Inte något (inte någonting)** | = **Inget (Ingenting)** fungerar. |
| fungerar.) | Nothing works. |
| (**Inte några** har varit här förut.) | = **Inga** har varit här förut. |
| | No one has been here before. |

When the negated phrase is the subject of a sub-clause, both alternatives are possible:

Jag vet, att **inte någon** kan komma = Jag vet att **ingen** kan komma
imorgon.                                                          imorgon.
I know that no one can come tomorrow.

Jag hoppas, att **inte något (inte nå-** = Jag hoppas att **inget (ingenting)**
**gonting)** tråkigt kommer att hända.   tråkigt kommer att hända.
I hope that nothing unfortunate will happen.

Note that **inte någon** is also used to refer to one of two, where English uses 'neither':

**Inte någon** av hans föräldrar var där. Neither of his parents was there.

Note also that **inte någon** used before a countable noun usually corresponds to 'not ... a' in English:

Han har **inte någon** far.          He hasn't got a father.

When **ingen** is used before a noun, it usually corresponds to 'no' in English:

| | |
|---|---|
| Vi har **ingen** tid. | We have no time. |
| Det finns **inget** intresse. | There is no interest. |
| Det finns **inga** nyheter. | There is no news. |

As with **någon, något (någonting)** and **några, ingen, inget (ingenting)** and **inga** can be used by themselves to mean 'nobody' ('no one'), 'nothing' and 'none':

| | |
|---|---|
| **Ingen** har varit här. | No one has been here. |
| **Inget (Ingenting)** har hänt. | Nothing has happened. |
| **Inga** av mina vänner har ringt. | None of my friends have rung. |

## 13.5 *all, hel, annan, sådan* and other determiners

Other common determiners have the following forms:

| SINGULAR | | PLURAL AND | |
|---|---|---|---|
| *'En' words* | *'Ett' words* | DEFINITE | |
| all | allt | all**a** | all |
| hel | hel**t** | hel**a** | whole |
| annan | annat | **andra** | another, other |
| sådan | sådan**t** | sådan**a** | such |

Here are some examples with comments on the use of these words:

**Hel (helt, hela)** 'whole' can only be used with countable nouns (10.4). When the noun is in the indefinite singular, **hel** (**en** words) and **helt** (**ett** words) are used:

| | |
|---|---|
| Lisa åt upp en **hel** banan. | Lisa ate up a whole banana. |
| Jan åt upp ett **helt** äpple. | Jan ate up a whole apple. |

With nouns in the definite form, **hela** is used. (Note that the article is not used, unless an adjective follows. In that case the definite article comes after **hela.**):

| | |
|---|---|
| Jag har väntat **hela** kvällen. | I have been waiting the whole evening. |
| **Hela** semestern var vi i Grekland. | We were in Greece (for) the whole holiday. |
| **Hela den** vackra stranden var täckt av olja. | The whole of the beautiful beach was covered with oil. |

In the plural **hela** is used even when the noun is indefinite:

| | |
|---|---|
| Vi har väntat två **hela** månader. | We have waited two whole months. |

**all, allt, alla** 'all'. With uncountable nouns (10.4) **all** is used with **en** words and **allt** with **ett** words:

| | |
|---|---|
| **All** ost och **allt** smör är slut. | All the cheese and all the butter is finished. |
| Jag sålde **all** min jord och **allt** annat som jag ägde. | I sold all my land and everything else I owned. |
| **Alla** de här bilarna måste tvättas. | All these cars have to be washed. |

Note that **alla** (= **alla människor**) corresponds to 'everybody', 'everyone' and **allt, allting** to 'all', 'everything':

| | |
|---|---|
| **Alla** (**alla människor**) gillar musik. | Everybody likes music. |
| **Alla** kan inte vara nöjda. | Not everyone can be pleased. |
| **Allt** är inte guld som glimmar. | All is not gold that glitters. |
| **Allting** (**Allt**) kan inte köpas för pengar. | Not everything can be bought with money. |

**sådan** (**sådant, sådana**) (**sån, sånt, såna** in spoken Swedish) 'such', 'what a', 'like that'

| | |
|---|---|
| Vilken snygg bil du har! | What a smart car you've got! |
| En **sådan** vill jag också ha. | I'd like one like that. |
| Titta, vilket konstigt träd! | Look, what an odd tree! |
| Ett **sådant** har jag aldrig sett förut. | I've never seen one like that before. |
| Kalle och Lisa är väldigt generösa. | Kalle and Lisa are terribly generous. |
| **Sådana** människor träffar man sällan. | You don't often meet people like that (such people). |
| Ge mig en **sådan!** | Give me one of those! |

**något sådant** (**nåt sånt** in spoken Swedish) 'something (anything) like that'

| | |
|---|---|
| Fick du verkligen en råtta i soppan? | Did you really get a mouse in your soup? |
| **Något sådant** har jag aldrig hört talas om. | I've never heard of anything like that. |

**(en) annan, (ett) annat, andra** 'another', 'other'. Note that Swedish uses the indefinite article (**en, ett**) when the noun is indefinite:

| | |
|---|---|
| Den här boken verkar tråkig. | This book seems boring. |
| Kan du låna mig **en annan?** | Can you lend me another one? |
| Det är fullt här. | We are full up. |
| Ni får gå till **ett annat** hotell. | You'll have to go to another hotel. |
| Har du **några andra** tidningar? | Have you got any other papers? |

Compare also:

| | |
|---|---|
| Du får be **någon annan** göra det. | You'll have to ask someone else to do it. |

110

**något annat** 'something (anything) else'

Vill du ha **något annat?**      Is there anything else you want?

**den ena (det ena), den andra (det andra), de andra** 'one', 'the other', 'the others'

| | |
|---|---|
| **Den ena** skon är brun och **den andra** (skon) är svart. | One shoe is brown and the other (shoe) is black. |
| **Det ena** snöret är för kort och **det andra** är för långt. | One lace is too short and the other is too long. |
| Ta inte de där strumporna. Ta **de andra.** | Don't take those socks. Take the others. |
| Nu måste vi gå. **De andra** väntar. | We must go now. The others are waiting. |

**Andra** can also mean 'second':

Det är **andra** dörren till vänster.      It's the second door on the left.

**en, två . . . till** 'another', 'two more'. To indicate that you want more of the same thing, you usually add the word **till** after the noun:

| | |
|---|---|
| Det här kaffet var gott. | This coffee is nice. |
| Kan jag få en kopp **till?** | Can I have another cup? |
| Jag har bara två skjortor. | I've only got two shirts. |
| Jag måste köpa några skjortor **till.** | I must buy some more shirts. |

You do not have to repeat the noun:

| | |
|---|---|
| Jag måste köpa några **till.** | I must buy some more. |
| Per hade bara en flaska öl hemma. | Per only had one bottle of beer at home. |
| Så han köpte fem (flaskor) **till.** | So he bought five more. |

**Varje** 'each', 'every' does not change its form. Nouns and adjectives after **varje** have the indefinite form:

| | |
|---|---|
| **Varje** människa behöver uppmuntran. | Every person needs encouragement. |
| Vi slutar kl. 3 **varje** fredag. | We close at 3 o'clock every Friday. |
| **Varje** år åker vi till England. | Every year we go to England. |
| **Varje** barn fick en present. | Each child got a present. |

**varannan, vartannat** 'every other'

| | |
|---|---|
| Han går på bio **varannan** vecka. | He goes to the cinema every other week. |
| Men jag går bara **vartannat** år. | But I only go every other year. |

**var tredje, fjärde ..., vart tredje, fjärde** 'every third, fourth'

| | |
|---|---|
| Jag är ledig **var tredje** dag. | I'm free every third day. |
| Han tar semester bara **vart tredje** år. | He only takes a holiday every third year. |
| Det går en buss **var femte** minut. | A bus goes every fifth minute (every five minutes). |
| **Vart fjärde** år är skottår. | Every fourth year is a leap-year. |

Note that nouns and adjectives are always in the indefinite form singular after **varje, varannan (vartannat)** and **var (vart) tredje** etc. (The difference between **en** words and **ett** words is kept, however.)

| | |
|---|---|
| **Varje** ny uppgift ska tas som en utmaning. | Each new task should be taken as a challenge. |
| **Varje** nytt år medför nya bekymmer. | Each new year brings new problems. |
| **Varannan** vit skjorta måste slängas. | Every other white shirt has to be thrown away. |
| **Vart tredje** nytt ord har jag glömt. | I have forgotten every third new word. |

# 14 Comparison. Comparative and superlative

## 14.1 General comments on comparison

Certain verbs can be used to compare different people or things:

**likna, vara lik** 'resemble', 'be like'

Maria **liknar** sin mamma. } Maria is like her mother.
Maria **är lik** sin mamma. }

**påminna om** 'remind (you) of'

Peter **påminner om** sin pappa.  Peter reminds you of his father.
(He looks a bit like his father.)

**se ut som** 'look like'

En zebra **ser ut som** en häst i    A zebra looks like a horse in
randig pyjamas.    striped pyjamas.

**låta som** 'sound like'

Jag **låter som** en hes kråka idag.    I sound like a hoarse crow today.

**kännas som** 'feel like'

Det här tyget **känns** mjukt **som**    This material feels as soft as silk.
silke.

Adjectives have special forms when you compare to what degree a certain quality occurs:

| | |
|---|---|
| Jan är lat. | Jan is lazy. |
| Peter är **lika** lat **som** Jan. | Peter is as lazy as Jan. |
| Men Eva är lat**are** än Jan. | But Eva is lazier than Jan. |
| Rune är lat**ast** av alla. | Rune is the laziest of all. |

If the quality occurs to the same degree, the words **lika** . . . **som** are used in Swedish, and 'as . . . as' in English.

In both Swedish and English the adjective has special forms when a quality occurs to a higher degree or to the highest degree. The form that denotes the higher degree is called the *comparative (komparativ)* and is formed by adding the ending **are** in Swedish and the ending 'er' in English. When a certain quality occurs to the highest degree the term *superlative (superlativ)* is used. The adjective in Swedish then has the ending **ast** and in English the ending 'est'. The adjective can thus have the following forms:

| BASIC FORM | COMPARATIVE<br>+ are | SUPERLATIVE<br>+ ast |
|---|---|---|
| stark<br>strong | starkare<br>stronger | starkast<br>strongest |
| snabb<br>quick | snabbare<br>quicker | snabbast<br>quickest |
| fri<br>free | friare<br>freer | friast<br>freest |
| dyr<br>dear, expensive | dyrare<br>dearer | dyrast<br>dearest |
| intelligent<br>intelligent | intelligentare<br>more intelligent | intelligentast<br>most intelligent |

As you can see from the last example, Swedish can use the endings **are** and **ast** even with long adjectives. However, there are certain adjectives that use a longer construction similar to the English 'more', 'most' construction. See 14.6.

Note the following constructions:

| | |
|---|---|
| Eva är **lika** stark **som** Peter. | Eva is as strong as Peter. |
| Men Karin är stark**are** **än** Eva. | But Karin is stronger than Eva. |

The same construction is used with the words **samma** 'same' and **annan** 'different':

| | |
|---|---|
| Bokhyllan har **samma** färg **som** bordet. | The bookcase is the same colour as the table. |
| Elsa arbetar på **samma** kontor **som** Anita. | Elsa works in the same office as Anita. |
| Stolarna har en **annan** färg **än** bordet. | The chairs are a different colour from the table. |
| Per arbetar på ett **annat** kontor **än** Jan. | Per works in a different office from Jan. |
| Elsa köper **andra** kläder **än** Anita. | Elsa buys different clothes from Anita. |

The word **samma** never changes its form. Note, too, that the noun that **samma** qualifies does not have an article or the definite form. The forms of **annan** are given in 13.5.

## 14.2 The comparative form of the adjective

It is easy to make the comparative form of adjectives. You just add **are** to the basic form:

| BASIC FORM | | | COMPARATIVE |
|---|---|---|---|
| lat<br>lazy | + are | → | lat**are**<br>lazier |
| varm<br>hot | + are | | varm**are**<br>hotter |
| kall<br>cold | + are | | kall**are**<br>colder |
| trött<br>tired | + are | | trött**are**<br>more tired |
| trevlig<br>nice | + are | | trevlig**are**<br>nicer |

A comparative never changes its form. Thus it has the same form with an **en** noun as with an **ett** noun in the singular or with a noun in the plural:

| | |
|---|---|
| Den här tröjan är **varmare** än den där. | This sweater is warmer than that one. |
| Det här huset är **varmare** än det där. | This house is warmer than that one. |
| De här långkalsongerna är **varmare** än de där. | These long-johns are warmer than those. |

An adjective in the comparative form can be used in various ways in a sentence:

| | |
|---|---|
| Kajsa är **trevligare** än Joakim. | Kajsa is nicer than Joakim. |
| Hon är **trevligare** på morgonen än på kvällen. | She is nicer in the morning than in the evening. |
| Du har ett **trevligare** jobb än jag. | You have a nicer job than me. |
| Det är **trevligare** att åka tåg än buss. | It is nicer to go by train than by bus. |
| Vi städar tillsammans. Det är **trevligare**. | Let's tidy up together. It's nicer. |

## 14.3 The superlative forms of the adjective

An adjective in the superlative has two forms. As well as the usual superlative form which ends in **ast** there is a special definite form which is formed by adding **e**:

| BASIC FORM | | | SUPERLATIVE | | | SUPERLATIVE DEFINITE FORM |
|---|---|---|---|---|---|---|
| lat<br>lazy | + ast | → | lat**ast**<br>laziest | + e | → | lat**aste**<br>laziest |
| varm<br>hot | + ast | | varm**ast**<br>hottest | + e | | varm**aste**<br>hottest |
| kall<br>cold | + ast | | kall**ast**<br>coldest | + e | | kall**aste**<br>coldest |
| trött<br>tired | + ast | | trött**ast**<br>most tired | + e | | trött**aste**<br>most tired |
| trevlig<br>nice | + ast | | trevlig**ast**<br>nicest | + e | | trevlig**aste**<br>nicest |

An adjective in the superlative can be used attributively and stand immediately in front of the noun it qualifies. In this case the definite form with **e** is always used. Note that the noun must also have the definite form and that there must be a definite article (**den, det, de**) in front of it (11.3).

| | |
|---|---|
| Det här är **den varmaste** tröjan. | This is the warmest sweater. |
| Det här är **det kallaste** rummet. | This is the coldest room. |
| Per och Eva är **de trevligaste**<br>människorna i min klass. | Per and Eva are the nicest<br>people in my class. |

If the noun is modified by a genitive or a possessive pronoun, the definite article before the noun and the definite form disappear. But the superlative must still have the definite form with **e**:

| | |
|---|---|
| Husets **trevligaste** rum ligger på<br>bottenvåningen. | The nicest room in the house is<br>on the bottom floor. |
| Rune är min **närmaste** vän. | Rune is my closest friend. |

When the superlative is used predicatively, you can choose between using the superlative form without **e** and the definite form with **e** preceded by the definite article (**den, det, de**):

| | |
|---|---|
| Den här tröjan är **varmast**.<br>Den här tröjan är **den varmaste**. | This sweater is the warmest. |
| Det här rummet är **kallast** i hela<br>lägenheten.<br>Det här rummet är **det kallaste** i<br>hela lägenheten. | This room is the coldest in the<br>whole flat. |
| Per och Eva är **trevligast** i min klass.<br>Per och Eva är **de trevligaste** i<br>min klass. | Per and Eva are the nicest (people)<br>in my class. |

116

When you compare something with itself, only the superlative form without **e** can be used. The word **som** can also be put in before the superlative:

| | |
|---|---|
| Nu är vintern (som) kall**ast**. | Now winter is (at its) coldest. |
| Compare: | |
| Den här vintern är **den kallaste** på länge. | This winter is the coldest for years. |
| På morgnarna är jag (som) **tröttast**. | I am most tired in the mornings. |
| På morgnarna är jag **den tröttaste** av alla på jobbet. | In the mornings I am the most tired person of all at work. |

## 14.4 Adjectives that end in *er, el* or *en*

Adjectives that end in an unstressed **e** followed by **r, l** or **n** lose the **e** when the endings **are** or **ast(e)** are added (compare 11.10).

| BASIC FORM | COMPARATIVE | SUPERLATIVE |
|---|---|---|
| vacker vack$e$r + **are** → beautiful | vackrare vack$e$r + **ast** → | vackrast(e) |
| säker säk$e$r sure | säkrare säk$e$r | säkrast(e) |
| enkel enk$e$l simple | enklare enk$e$l | enklast(e) |
| vaken vak$e$n awake | vaknare vak$e$n | vaknast(e) |

## 14.5 Irregular adjectives

There are certain adjectives which have irregular forms in the comparative and superlative. As these adjectives are among the commonest in the language, it pays to learn them in all their forms as quickly as possible:

| BASIC FORM | COMPARA-TIVE | SUPERLA-TIVE | SUPERLATIVE DEFINITE FORM |
|---|---|---|---|
| bra good | bättre better | bäst best | bästa |
| dålig bad | sämre worse | sämst worst | sämsta |
| liten small | mindre smaller, less | minst smallest, least | minsta |
| gammal old | äldre older, elder | äldst oldest, eldest | äldsta |

The words change in the comparative and superlative. The forms are not completely irregular, however, as the comparative ends in **re** and the superlative in **st**. The definite form of the superlative is formed by adding an **a** to the simple superlative form.

| | | | |
|---|---|---|---|
| Sten är **äldre** än Per. | | Sten is older than Per. | |
| Eva är **äldst (den äldsta)** av systrarna. | | Eva is the eldest of the sisters. | |
| De **äldsta** tavlorna är dyrast. | | The oldest pictures are the most expensive. | |
| Borta bra, men hemma **bäst**. | | East, west, home is best. (Proverb) | |

Another type of irregular adjective changes its vowel in the comparative and superlative. In the comparative the ending is **re** and in the superlative **st**. The definite form adds an **a** to the simple form of the superlative

| BASIC FORM | COMPARA-TIVE | SUPERLA-TIVE | SUPERLATIVE DEFINITE FORM |
|---|---|---|---|
| | *Vowel change* + **re** | *Vowel change* + **st** | + **a** |
| stor<br>big | stör**re** | stör**st** | störst**a** |
| grov<br>coarse | gröv**re** | gröv**st** | grövst**a** |
| lång<br>long, tall | läng**re** | läng**st** | längst**a** |
| låg<br>low | läg**re** | läg**st** | lägst**a** |
| ung<br>young | yng**re** | yng**st** | yngst**a** |
| tung<br>heavy | tyng**re** | tyng**st** | tyngst**a** |
| *Without vowel change:* | | | |
| hög<br>high | hög**re** | hög**st** | högst**a** |

| | |
|---|---|
| En liten elefant är **större** än en stor mygga. | A little elephant is bigger than a big mosquito. |
| Den som är **störst** är inte alltid starkast. | He who is biggest is not always strongest. |
| Vänern är Sveriges **största** sjö. | Vänern is Sweden's largest lake. |
| Karin är **längre** än Sten. | Karin is taller than Sten. |
| Sveriges kust är **längre** än Skottlands. | The coast of Sweden is longer than that of Scotland. |
| Olle har **längre** semester än Elsa. | Olle has a longer holiday than Elsa. |
| Temperaturen är **lägre** på natten än på dagen. | The temperature is lower at night than in the daytime. |
| Ola är inte **yngst**. Mats är **yngre**. | Ola isn't the youngest. Mats is younger. |

## 14.6 Making the comparative and the superlative with *mer* and *mest*

As in English, certain adjectives cannot take an ending in the comparative and superlative. Instead they take the word **mer** 'more' to make the comparative and the word **mest** 'most' to make the superlative:

| | |
|---|---|
| Eva är **mer** energisk än Peter. | Eva is more energetic than Peter. |
| Olle är **mest** sympatisk av mina grannar. | Olle is the most likeable of my neighbours. |
| Kristina är **mer** cynisk än Ann. | Kristina is more cynical than Ann. |

This is the rule:

---

Adjectives that end in **isk** and present and past participles form the comparative and superlative with **mer** and **mest**.

---

As in English, there is also a tendency to choose the forms with **mer** and **mest** with long adjectives, which would become very heavy with the **are** and **ast** endings:

| | |
|---|---|
| Han är Sveriges mest framgångsrika affärsman. | He is Sweden's most successful businessman. |
| Det vore den mest lyckosamma lösningen. | It would be the happiest solution. |

Adjectives and past participles change their forms in the usual way (11.8) when they come after **mer** and **mest**. Present participles, however, never change their form (9.14).

| | |
|---|---|
| Han blev mer energisk med åren. | He became more energetic as the years passed. |
| De blev mer energiska med åren. | They became more energetic as the years passed. |
| Eva blev mer och mer irriterad. | Eva got more and more irritated. |
| Men mest irriterade var hennes vänner. | But the most irritated people were her friends. |
| Peter är mer förstående än Olle. | Peter is more understanding than Olle. |

## 14.7 Adverbs. Words denoting degree, quantity and number

Many adverbs can also be compared, particularly those that denote manner (compare 2.8). If the adverb is formed from an adjective, it usually has the same forms as the adjective in the comparative and superlative:

| | |
|---|---|
| Peter sjunger inte lika **vackert** som Eva. | Peter doesn't sing as beautifully as Eva. |
| Hon sjunger **vackrare**. | She sings more beautifully. |
| Men allra **vackrast** sjunger Rolf. | But Rolf sings most beautifully of all. |

Words that denote degree, quantity and number often have special forms in the comparative and superlative. Note also the adverb **gärna** 'gladly':

| BASIC FORM | COMPARA- TIVE | SUPERLA- TIVE | SUPERLATIVE DEFINITE FORM |
|---|---|---|---|
| mycket <br> much, very | mer <br> more | mest <br> most | mesta |
| lite <br> a little | mindre <br> less | minst <br> least | minsta |
| många <br> many | fler <br> more | flest <br> most | flesta |
| få <br> few | färre <br> fewer | – | – |
| gärna <br> gladly | hellre <br> rather | helst <br> rather, preferably | – |
| nära <br> close, near | närmare <br> closer | närmast <br> closest | närmaste <br> closest |

| | |
|---|---|
| Sten åt bara lite gröt. | Sten only ate a little porridge. |
| Han åt till och med **mindre** än Karin. | He even ate less than Karin. |
| Gustav arbetar **mindre** än Helen, men han tjänar **mer** än hon. | Gustav works less than Helen, but he earns more than she does. |
| Per arbetar **minst** och pratar **mest**. | Per works least and talks most. |
| Det går alltför **få** bussar på natten. | There are far too few buses at night. |
| Det går **färre** bussar på natten än på dagen. | There are fewer buses at night than in the daytime. |
| Du får **gärna** låna mitt kastspö. | You are welcome to borrow my fishing rod. |
| Jag gillar inte att arbeta på helgerna. Jag jobbar **hellre** över någon dag i veckan. | I don't like working at the weekends. I would rather work late on a weekday. |
| Eva är en **nära** vän till min syster. | Eva is a close friend of my sister's. |
| Bor du **närmare** busshållplatsen än jag? | Do you live closer to the bus stop than I do? |
| Är det här **närmaste** vägen till stationen? | Is this the shortest way to the station? |

# 15 Expressions of place. Position and direction

In this chapter we shall be describing place expressions of various kinds: how to say where someone or something is, where something happens, where someone comes from or where someone goes and similar expressions. A distinction is usually made between position and direction. Expressions of *position (befintlighet)* answer the question *Where? (Var?)*. Expressions of *direction (riktning)* answer the questions *Where ... to? (Vart?)* and *Where ... from? (Varifrån?)*.

## 15.1 *här* and *där*

Some of the most important place expressions consist of only one word. The commonest of them are shown in the table below:

| POSITION | DIRECTION | |
|---|---|---|
| *Where?* | *Where ... to?* | *Where ... from?* |
| här | hit | härifrån |
| here | here | from here |
| där | dit | därifrån |
| there | there | from there |

As you can see, Swedish distinguishes between position and direction with these words more clearly than English does.

Here is a dialogue to show you how these words are used:

*A telephone conversation*

– Hej! Det är Peter.

– Hej! Var är du? Jag trodde att du skulle komma **hit.**

– Jovisst. Men jag är kvar **här** i Malmö. Jag missade tåget. Jag åker **härifrån** om en timme. Kan du möta mig på Centralen? Jag bör vara **där** kl. 10.

– Men kan du inte ta en taxi **därifrån?** Det kostar inte så mycket.

– Jovisst. Men kan du inte komma **dit**, så kan vi promenera tillsammans? Det är trevligare.

– Okay då. Men missa inte tåget den här gången!

– Hallo. It's Peter.

– Hallo. Where are you? I thought you were coming here.

– That's right. But I'm still here in Malmö. I missed the train. I'm leaving here in an hour. Can you meet me at the Central Station? I should be there at 10 o'clock.

– But can't you take a taxi from there? It doesn't cost much.

– Sure. But can't you go there, then we can walk together? That's nicer.

– OK. But don't miss the train this time!

121

## 15.2 Verbs denoting position

The verb **vara** 'be' can be used, as in English, together with an expression of place that denotes position:

| | |
|---|---|
| Var är Olle? | Where's Olle? |
| Han är i köket. | He's in the kitchen. |
| Var är boken? | Where's the book? |
| Den ligger på bordet. | It's on the table. |

In the answer to the last question Swedish uses the verb **ligga** 'lie' instead of **vara**. It is not completely impossible to say: **Den är på bordet.** But that is not the usual way of saying it in Swedish. Swedish uses the verbs **sitta** 'sit', **stå** 'stand' and **ligga** 'lie' to describe the position of people, animals, things and places. Both Swedish and English use these verbs together with an expression of place to describe people and animals:

| | |
|---|---|
| Eva **sitter** vid bordet. | Eva is sitting at the table. |
| Pojkarna **står** på gården. | The boys are standing in the yard. |
| Rolf **ligger** i sängen. | Rolf is lying in bed. |

Occasionally in English, but regularly in Swedish, the verb **stå** 'stand' is used to describe an object that has a vertical position, and the verb **ligga** 'lie' when the object has a horizontal position:

| | |
|---|---|
| Vasen **står** på bordet. | The vase is (standing) on the table. |
| (The normal expression) | |
| Vasen **ligger** på bordet. | The vase is lying on the table. |
| (If it has fallen over) | |
| Boken **står** i bokhyllan. | The book is in the bookcase. |
| (The normal position) | |
| Boken **ligger** på bordet. | The book is on the table. |
| (It is flat on the table) | |

There is an important group of words for everyday things of various kinds which are thought to have a definite top and bottom:

| | |
|---|---|
| Bilen **står** i garaget. | The car is (standing) in the garage. |
| Soffan **står** i vardagsrummet. | The sofa is in the living room. |
| Stereon **står** på en ölback. | The stereo is on a beer crate. |
| Tallriken **står** på bordet. | The plate is on the table. |

You say, for example, that a car **står** in the garage when its wheels are on the ground and the roof, 'the top', is upward. You can also use the verb **ligga** about objects like this, but then you know that they are not in their normal position, but on their side, for example:

| | |
|---|---|
| Bilen **ligger** i diket. | The car is (lying) in the ditch. |

Compare these two examples:

Skorna **står** i hallen.  The shoes are in the hall.
Skorna **ligger** i hallen.  The shoes are in the hall.

You use the verb **stå** when the shoes are there with their soles and heels on the floor, that is to say in their normal position. The verb **ligga** is used if the shoes are on their sides or upside down or placed untidily.

For objects like carpets and clothes you can usually only use **ligga** 'lie':

Mattan **ligger** i sovrummet.  The carpet is in the bedroom.

When you use the verbs **stå** and **ligga** you usually mean that the objects are not fixed in position. The verb **sitta** is used about things that are fastened or fixed in position.

Compare the following examples:

Räkningarna **sitter** i pärmen.  The bills are in the file.
(If the bills are filed away)
Räkningarna **ligger** i pärmen.  The bills are in the file.
(If they are lying loose)
Det **sitter** en spegel i hallen.*  There's a mirror in the hall.
(Hanging on the wall)
Det **står** en spegel i hallen.  There's a mirror in the hall.
(Standing on the floor)
Löven **sitter** fortfarande kvar  The leaves are still on the trees.
på träden.
Höstlöven **ligger** på marken.  The autumn leaves are lying on the ground.

The verb **ligga** has another special use not covered by the examples above. **Ligga** is used in the sense of 'is situated' about places and often about buildings, too:

Stockholm **ligger** ganska nära  Stockholm is fairly close to
Uppsala.  Uppsala.
Malmö **ligger** i Skåne.  Malmö is in Skåne.
Villan **ligger** nere vid sjön.  The house is down by the lake.

Note that when one of these three verbs is combined with another verb, the construction is different from English. In Swedish the verbs are joined with **och** and they are both in the same tense. Sometimes the verbs **sitta, stå** and **ligga** are not translated into English in these constructions.

Per **sitter och läser.**  Per is (sitting) reading.
Per **satt och läste** när vi kom.  Per was reading when we came.
Per har **suttit och läst.**  Per has been (sitting) reading.

* This **det** construction is explained in Chapter 17.

Here are a few more examples:

| | |
|---|---|
| Gun **ligger och sover.** | Gun is asleep. |
| Hon **låg** i sängen **och lyssnade** | She lay in bed listening to |
| på radion, innan hon somnade. | the radio before she fell asleep. |
| Rolf **stod och diskade** i köket. | Rolf was doing the washing up |
| | in the kitchen. |
| Pojkarna **står** på gården **och** | The boys are (standing) in the |
| **pratar** om fotboll. | yard talking about football. |
| Eva **sitter** vid bordet **och läser** | Eva is sitting at the table, |
| en tidning. | reading a newspaper. |

## 15.3 Prepositions denoting position

In this section we shall be going through the most important prepositions that denote position. Compare the following examples:

| | |
|---|---|
| Stolen står **vid** skåpet. | The chair is next to the cupboard. |
| Boken ligger **på** skåpet. | The book is on the cupboard. |
| Boken ligger **i** skåpet. | The book is in the cupboard. |
| Eva bor **hos** sin bror. | Eva lives with her brother. |

The preposition **vid** 'by', 'at', 'next to' denotes position next to something without there necessarily being any contact.

| | |
|---|---|
| Familjen Nygren sitter **vid** bordet | The Nygrens are sitting at the |
| och äter. | table eating. |
| Vi bor **vid** biblioteket. | We live by the library. |
| Elsa stannade **vid** en kiosk och | Elsa stopped at a kiosk and |
| köpte en korv. | bought a hot-dog. |

The preposition **på** 'on' denotes position on something that is seen as a line or a surface (for example, a table top, a wall, a floor). In contrast to **vid** it denotes contact.

| | |
|---|---|
| Babyn sitter **på** bordet. | The baby is sitting on the table. |
| Tavlan hänger **på** väggen. | The picture is hanging on the wall. |
| Glöm inte att skriva adressen | Don't forget to write the address |
| **på** brevet. | on the envelope. |

The preposition **i** 'in' is used mainly about position in something that is seen to have volume (a house, a room, various containers: a bag, a bottle, a pocket, etc.)

| | |
|---|---|
| Elsa duschar **i** badrummet. | Elsa is having a shower in the |
| | bathroom. |
| Vad har du **i** väskan? | What have you got in the bag? |

The preposition **hos** is used when somebody is staying or living in someone else's house, etc. It corresponds to the French preposition *chez* and the English equivalents are 'with' or 'at X's (house)', or some other preposition:

| | |
|---|---|
| Barnen är **hos** en granne. | The children are with a neighbour. |
| Jag bodde **hos** min farmor. | I lived at my grandmother's. |
| Jag arbetade **hos** en läkare innan jag gifte mig. | I worked for a doctor before I got married. |
| Hur var det **hos** doktorn? | How was it at the doctor's? |

Note the following very important special uses:

**1.** Countries, towns, villages: **i**

| | |
|---|---|
| Maj bor **i** Bromma och Allan bor **i** Västerås. | Maj lives in Bromma and Allan lives in Västerås. |
| Amsterdam är en stad **i** Holland. | Amsterdam is a town in Holland. |
| Vi stannade **i** en liten by. | We stopped in (at) a small village. |

Swedish always uses **i** about places, however small they are, where English can use 'at', especially about small places.

**2.** Islands: **på**

| | |
|---|---|
| Vi hade semester **på** Island. | We had a holiday on Iceland. |
| Maria har ett hotell **på** Kreta. | Maria has a hotel on (in) Crete. |

Swedish always uses **på** about islands, however large, while English sometimes uses 'in' rather than 'on' about large islands.

**3.** Addresses: **på**

| | |
|---|---|
| Jag bor **på** Storgatan 12, 2 tr (= trappor). | I live at Storgatan 18, on the second floor. |
| Restaurangen ligger **på** Kungsgatan. | The restaurant is in Kungsgatan. |

Swedish uses **på** both about streets and about addresses, while English uses 'at' with an address including a house number and 'in' for a street alone. Note: **på gatan** 'in the street'.

**4.** Places where you carry on a particular activity: **på**

The preposition **på** is used instead of **i** about places where you carry on a special activity. This mainly concerns places of work, places where you do certain business (the post office, banks) or where you go for entertainment (the theatre, the cinema).

| | |
|---|---|
| Han jobbar **på** ett sjukhus/**på** en verkstad/**på** ett bage**ri**. | He works in a hospital/a workshop/ a bakery. |
| Eva jobbar **på** posten nu. Förut jobbade hon **på** en bank. | Eva works at the post office now. She used to work at a bank. |
| Den här boken har jag lånat **på** biblioteket. | I borrowed this book from the library. |
| Ska vi gå **på** bio eller ska vi gå **på** diskotek? | Shall we go to the cinema or to a disco? |
| Vi träffas **på** bio. | Let's meet at the cinema. |

*Exceptions:* **i skolan, i affären, i kyrkan**

| | |
|---|---|
| Karin måste gå **i** skolan i nio år. | Karin has to go to school for nine years. |
| De går **i** kyrkan varje söndag. | They go to church every Sunday. |
| Josefin träffar ofta Olle **i** affären. | Josefin often meets Olle at (in) the shop. |

## 15.4 Prepositions denoting direction

Two of the most important prepositions that denote direction are **till** 'to' and **från** 'from'. **Till** is used in answer to the question **Vart?** 'Where . . . to?' and **från** in answer to the question **Varifrån?** 'Where . . . from ?':

| *Varifrån?* | *Vart?* |
|---|---|
| Eva flög **från** Stockholm. | Hon reste **till** London. |
| Eva flew from Stockholm. | She travelled to London. |
| Per simmade **från** båten | **till** ön. |
| Per swam from the boat | to the island. |

Here are some more examples:

| | |
|---|---|
| Vi åkte tåg **från** Stockholm **till** Göteborg. | We went by train from Stockholm to Gothenburg. |
| Familjen Persson åkte bil **från** Malmö **till** Västerås. | The Perssons went by car from Malmö to Västerås. |
| Jag måste gå **till** doktorn. | I must go to the doctor's. |
| Han kommer just **från** tandläkaren. | He has just come back from the dentist's. |

There are a few more prepositions that denote direction or movement:

**genom** 'through'

| | |
|---|---|
| Vi promenerade **genom** parken. | We walked through the park. |
| Göta Älv flyter **genom** Göteborg. | The river Göta flows through Gothenburg. |

**längs** 'along'

| | |
|---|---|
| Stigen går **längs** stranden. | The path runs along the beach. |

**över** 'across', 'over'

| | |
|---|---|
| Björn simmade **över** floden. | Björn swam across the river. |
| Planet flög **över** vårt hus. | The plane flew over our house. |

**mot** 'towards', 'to'

| | |
|---|---|
| De seglade **mot** Gotland. | They sailed towards Gotland. |
| Floderna flyter **mot** havet. | The rivers run down to the sea. |

126

## 15.5 Some important verbs of motion

To describe movement by means of some sort of vehicle or other means of transport Swedish uses the verbs **resa** 'go', 'travel', **åka** 'go', 'travel' and **köra** 'drive'.

**Resa** is mainly used about long journeys:

| | |
|---|---|
| Familjen **reser** utomlands varje sommar. | The family goes (travels) abroad every summer. |
| Jag **reste** med tåg och båt från Stockholm till London. | I went (travelled) by train and boat from Stockholm to London. |

**Åka** is the verb with the most general meaning. It can be used about long journeys (instead of **resa**) as well as short ones:

| | |
|---|---|
| Familjen **åker** utomlands varje sommar. | The family goes (travels) abroad every summer. |
| Jag **åker** buss till jobbet kl. 7 på morgonen. | I go to work by bus at 7 o'clock in the morning. |
| Ska vi **åka** och bada? | Shall we go for a swim? |

**Köra** is only used about a driver. Compare the following examples:

| | |
|---|---|
| Barnen **åker** bil till skolan. | The children go to school by car. |
| Deras pappa **kör** dem i sin bil. | Their father takes (drives) them in his car. |
| Jan **kör** buss. Han är busschaufför. | Jan drives a bus. He is a bus driver. |

**Köra** is used particularly about cars, lorries, etc. **Åka** is always used in the following expressions:

**åka skidor** 'ski'

| | |
|---|---|
| På vintern kan man **åka skidor**. | In the winter you can ski. |

**åka skridskor** 'skate'

| | |
|---|---|
| Eller också kan man **åka skridskor**. | Or you can skate. |

**åka cykel, cykla** 'ride a bike', 'cycle'

| | |
|---|---|
| Per **åker cykel** till jobbet. }<br>Per **cyklar** till jobbet. } | Per cycles to work. |

Note that the word that describes the means of transport does not have an article when it is used as a kind of object after the verbs **åka** and **köra**. After the verb **resa** the preposition **med** is put before the means of transportation:

| resa | ⎧ med båt<br>⎨ med flyg<br>⎩ med tåg<br>   med buss | go | ⎧ by boat<br>⎨ by plane<br>⎩ by train<br>   by bus |
|---|---|---|---|
| åka | ⎧ båt<br>⎪ flyg<br>⎨ tåg<br>⎪ buss<br>⎪ bil<br>⎩ cykel | go by | ⎧ boat<br>⎪ plane<br>⎨ train<br>⎪ bus<br>⎪ car<br>⎩ bike |

127

|  | | |  | | |
|---|---|---|---|---|---|
| **köra** | traktor<br>buss<br>bil<br>motorcykel<br>moped | | drive<br>(ride) | a tractor<br>a bus<br>a car<br>a motorbike<br>a moped | |

Vi **reste med** buss till Göteborg. }
Vi **åkte** buss till Göteborg.

We went by bus to Gothenburg.

Han får **köra** motorcykel och bil, men han får inte **köra** lastbil ännu.

He can drive a motorbike or a car, but he is not allowed to drive a lorry yet.

Note that the Swedish verb **rida** is used only about horse-riding:

Min lillasyster kunde **rida** innan hon kunde **cykla**.

My little sister could ride a horse before she could ride a bicycle.

**skjutsa** 'drive', 'give a lift'
**frakta** 'take', 'carry'

Instead of **köra** you can use **skjutsa** if the verb has an object that is a person. If the object is a thing, goods, etc., you can use **frakta** instead:

Jag kan **skjutsa (köra)** dig hem i min bil.

I can drive you (give you a lift) home in my car.

Eva **fraktade (körde)** hem de nya möblerna i en skåpbil.

Eva took the new furniture home in a van.

The verb **gå** corresponds to both 'go' and 'walk' in English. Note that if you use **gå** about a person in Swedish, it always means that he walks, goes on foot. Compare the following examples:

Min fru måste **åka** tunnelbana till jobbet.

My wife has to go to work by underground.

Men min arbetsplats ligger så nära att jag kan **gå.**

But my office is so close that I can walk.

Vi **gick** från London till Brighton.

We walked from London to Brighton.

Vi **åkte** från London till Brighton.

We went (drove, etc.) from London to Brighton.

**Gå** can also be used to mean 'leave':

Är Björn här?

Is Björn here?

Nej, han har redan **gått.**

No, he has already left (gone).

To convey the same meaning you can use either **ge sig av** 'leave', which is a little more formal or **sticka** 'push off', which is more or less slang:

Gästerna har redan **gett sig av.**

The guests have already left.

Nu **sticker** vi.

We're pushing off now.

**Gå** can also be used about trains, buses, boats and planes:

Det här tåget (Den här bussen)     This train (This bus) goes to
**går** till flygplatsen.     the airport.
Båten **går** inte förrän kl. 9.     The boat doesn't leave until
    9 o'clock.

# 15.6 Verbs corresponding to 'put'

The English verb 'put' corresponds to three verbs in Swedish: **sätta, ställa** and **lägga**.

**Ställa** is used when you place something in an upright position (corresponds to **stå**, see 15.2):

Ola **ställde** vasen på bordet.     Ola put the vase on the table.
Compare:
Vasen **står** på bordet.     The vase is (standing) on the table.
Jag **ställer** paraplyet mot väggen.     I'll put (stand) the umbrella
    against the wall.

Compare:
Paraplyet **står** mot väggen.     The umbrella is standing against
    the wall.
Vem har **ställt** bilen i garaget?     Who has put the car in the garage?

**Lägga** is used when you place something in a horizontal position (corresponds to **ligga**, see 15.2):

Jag **lägger** paraplyet på bordet.     I'll put (lay) the umbrella on
    the table.

Compare:
Paraplyet **ligger** på bordet.     The umbrella is (lying) on the table.
Någon har **lagt** en duk på bordet.     Someone has put (laid) a cloth on
    the table.

Compare:
Det **ligger** en duk på bordet.     There is a cloth on the table.

**Sätta** is used when you fasten something somewhere (corresponds to **sitta**, see 15.2):

Jag **sätter** räkningarna i pärmen.     I'll put the bills in the file.
Compare:
Räkningarna **sitter** i pärmen.     The bills are in the file.
Peter har **satt** upp gardiner i     Peter has put up curtains in
köket.     the kitchen.
Compare:
Det **sitter** gardiner i köket.     There are curtains in the kitchen.

Sätta can also be used instead of ställa, and then it usually indicates that something is placed so that it is in the right place, where it belongs:

| | |
|---|---|
| Ställ tallrikarna på bordet | Put the plates on the table. |
| = Sätt tallrikarna på bordet. | |
| Jag ställde bilen i garaget. | I put the car in the garage. |
| = Jag satte bilen i garaget. | |

In such cases you cannot use sitta about the object, but only stå:

| | |
|---|---|
| Tallrikarna står på bordet. | The plates are on the table. |
| *Wrong:* Tallrikarna sitter på bordet. | |

Two somewhat similar verbs are stoppa 'put', 'stick' and hänga 'hang'.

Stoppa is used when you place something in something:

| | |
|---|---|
| Jag stoppade handen i fickan. | I put my hand in my pocket. |
| Du får inte stoppa kniven i munnen när du äter. | You mustn't put (stick) your knife in your mouth when you eat. |
| Vi hängde tavlan i hallen. | We hung the picture in the hall. |
| Compare: | |
| Tavlan hänger i hallen. | The picture is (hanging) in the hall. |

Compare how the verbs sätta, ställa and lägga are used about people:

| | |
|---|---|
| Ulla satte sig på stolen. | Ulla sat down on the chair. |
| Mats ställde sig vid dörren. | Mats (walked over and) stood by the door. |
| Jan la(de) sig i sängen. | Jan lay down on the bed |

## 15.7 Preposition of position instead of preposition of direction

Note the following expressions where Swedish uses a preposition of position instead of a preposition of direction:

| | |
|---|---|
| Kan du hämta en penna på mitt skrivbord? | Can you fetch a pen from my desk? |
| Per hämtade barnen på dagis. | Per fetched the children from the day nursery. |
| Jag lånade den här boken på biblioteket. | I borrowed this book from the library. |
| Vi går på bio varje fredag. | We go to the cinema every Friday. |
| Vi går på teater alltför sällan. | We go to the theatre far too seldom. |
| Förr i tiden gick de flesta i kyrkan på söndagarna. | Most people used to go to church on Sundays. |

130

# 15.8 Particles

In Swedish as in English there are a number of particles which are used to denote position. Note that these particles, unlike prepositions, are stressed (compare 9.17).

Here are the most important particles:

| POSITION | DIRECTION | |
|---|---|---|
| *Where?* | *Where to?* | *Where from?* |
| hemma | hem | hemifrån |
| at home | home | from home |
| borta | bort | bortifrån |
| away | away | from a long way away |
| inne | in | inifrån |
| inside, indoors | in, inside, indoors | from inside |
| ute | ut | utifrån |
| outside, outdoors | out, outside, outdoors | from outside |
| uppe | upp | uppifrån |
| up (there) | up | from above |
| nere | ner, ned | nerifrån |
| down (there) | down | from below |
| framme | fram | framifrån |
| in front (here) | forward, on | from the front |

| | |
|---|---|
| Sten är ensam **hemma**. Föräldrarna är **borta** hos en bekant. | Sten is alone at home. His parents are away at a friend's. |
| Eva måste gå **hemifrån** kl. 7 varje morgon. | Eva has to leave home at 7 o'clock every morning. |
| Hon kommer **hem** kl. 6. | She gets home at 6 o'clock. |
| Maria står **inne** i köket och tittar **ut** genom fönstret. | Maria is standing in the kitchen looking out through the window. |
| **Ute** på gården leker några barn, som kastar **upp** stenar i luften. | Out in the yard some children are playing, throwing stones up in the air. |
| Gå **in** genom den högra dörren och **ut** genom den vänstra! | Go in through the right-hand door and out through the left-hand one. |
| Olle bor **uppe** på vinden. | Olle lives up in the attic. |
| Vi förvarar allt gammalt skräp **nere** i källaren. | We keep all the old rubbish down in the cellar. |

When you talk about places on a map, **uppe** and **nere** are often used in a special way, just as in English. **Uppe** is used about places north of the place you are in, and **nere** about places south of where you are:

| | |
|---|---|
| De bor **nere** i Malmö. | They live down in Malmö. |
| Sommaren tillbringar de **uppe** i fjällen. | They spend the summer up in the mountains. |
| Jag tänker åka **ner** till Göteborg i övermorgon. | I am going down to Gothenburg the day after tomorrow. |

**tillbaka** 'back'

| | |
|---|---|
| Jag går nu. Jag kommer **tillbaka** om en timme. | I'm going now. I'll be back in an hour. |
| Du måste lämna **tillbaka** böckerna till biblioteket. | You must take the books back to the library. |
| Kan du ge **tillbaka** på en hundralapp? | Can you change a hundred crown note? |

**bak – bakåt – baklänges**

| | |
|---|---|
| Han gick **baklänges** in i rummet. | He walked backwards into the room. |
| Han gick **bakåt** i bussen. | He went to the back of the bus. |
| Han satt längst **bak** i bussen. | He sat right at the back of the bus. |

## 15.9 *'Pojken sprang in i huset/ut ur huset'*

Swedish sometimes uses a particle denoting direction together with a preposition that denotes position (for example **i** 'in', **på** 'at', 'on') when one might have expected **till** 'to' to have been used. Compare the following examples:

| | |
|---|---|
| Vi gick **till** parken. | We went to the park. |
| Vi gick **in i** parken. | We went into (entered) the park. |
| Flickan simmade **till** grottan. | The girl swam to the cave. |
| Flickan simmade **in i** grottan. | The girl swam into the cave. |

As you can see, movement into a place is expressed by **in i**. In the same way, movement out of a place is expressed by **ut ur**:

| | |
|---|---|
| Vi gick **ut ur** parken. | We left (went out of) the park. |
| Flickan simmade **ut ur** grottan. | The girl swam out of the cave. |

A particle denoting direction can also be combined with the preposition **på**:

| | |
|---|---|
| Katten hoppade **upp på** bordet. | The cat jumped up onto the table. |

For movement away from the place where you are, however, the preposition **från** is used, with a particle:

| | |
|---|---|
| Katten hoppade **ner från** bordet. | The cat jumped down from the table. |

Compare the following set of examples:

| | |
|---|---|
| Bilen stod **i** garaget. | The car was in the garage. |
| Karin körde **in** bilen **i** garaget. | Karin drove the car into the garage. |
| Karin körde **ut** bilen **ur** garaget. | Karin drove the car out of the garage. |
| Pojken sprang omkring **inne i** huset. | The boy was running about in (inside) the house. |
| Pojken sprang **in i** huset. | The boy ran into the house. |
| Pojken sprang **ut ur** huset. | The boy ran out of the house. |
| Lådan stod **på** bordet. | The box was on the table. |
| Jag lyfte **upp** lådan **på** bordet. | I lifted the box on to the table. |
| Jag lyfte **ner** lådan **från** bordet. | I lifted the box down from (off) the table. |

# 16 Subordinate clauses and infinitive constructions

This chapter presents a more detailed description of the structure of *subordinate clauses (bisatser)*. We suggest you start by looking again at the section on subordinate clauses in Chapter 7.

Note, too, the many examples of verbs that can be combined with subordinate clauses and infinitive expressions in various ways. Many of these verbs have abstract meanings; they are constructed in special ways and they are not always easy to understand.

Another aim of this chapter is to help you to build up your vocabulary.

## 16.1 The infinitive marker *att*

The use of the infinitive of the verb after certain auxiliary verbs is described in 6.1–6.3. Infinitive expressions can also be used as subject and object in clauses of the following kinds in which the infinitive functions rather like a noun:

| | |
|---|---|
| Att simma är roligt. | Swimming is fun. |
| (Infinitive as subject) | |
| Compare: | |
| Simning är roligt. | Swimming is fun. |
| (Noun as subject) | |
| Lena älskar att simma. | Lena loves to swim. |
| (Infinitive as object) | |
| Compare: | |
| Lena älskar simning. | Lena loves swimming. |
| (Noun as object) | |

In expressions of this kind the infinitive form of the verb takes the infinitive marker **att** 'to'. Normally this has to be placed before a verb in the infinitive in Swedish. It is only after certain verbs that it is never used. (This applies chiefly to the verbs presented in 6.3.)

The infinitive marker **att** has the same written form as the **att** which corresponds to English 'that' and introduces **att** clauses, as in the following example:

| | |
|---|---|
| Vi såg, att Lena simmade i viken. | We saw that Lena was swimming in the bay. |

In the spoken language there is often a difference between the infinitive marker **att** and the **att** which corresponds to 'that': the infinitive marker is often pronounced **å**, but this form is not used in writing.

Lena älskar **att** simma = Lena älskar **å** simma. (Only spoken Swedish)

The **att** which introduces **att** clauses can never be pronounced **å**; it is pronounced as it is spelt. Note that a comma is never placed before the infinitive marker **att** (compare 7.3).

As in English, an infinitive expression cannot have a subject of its own, but an infinitive can, of course, be combined with an object and an adverbial in the same way as an ordinary verb can:

| | |
|---|---|
| Lena tycker om att **dansa** vals. | Lena likes to dance the waltz. |
| Hon har lovat att **dansa** med mig ikväll. | She has promised to dance with me this evening. |

Thus the following rules govern the use of the infinitive:

---

The infinitive marker **att** is normally placed in front of a verb in the infinitive.
No subject is placed before a verb in the infinitive.

---

Note the exception to the rule that **att** is placed in front of a verb in the infinitive:

---

**Att** is not used after the following auxiliary verbs:

| | | |
|---|---|---|
| **måste** 'must', | **kunna** 'be able', | **ska** 'shall', 'will', 'should',' would' |
| **vilja** 'want', | **få** 'be allowed', | **tänka** 'think' |
| **bör** 'ought to', 'should' | **behöva** 'need' | **bruka** 'be in the habit' |

---

These verbs are described in more detail in 6.3, apart from **tänka**, which is presented in 9.2.

| | |
|---|---|
| Lena **kan** simma. | Lena can swim. |
| Lena **måste** dansa vals med mig ikväll. | Lena must dance a waltz with me this evening. |
| Jag **skall** hjälpa dig. | I will help you. |
| Vi **vill** inte förlora en match till. | We don't want to lose another match. |
| **Får** jag komma in? | May I come in? |
| Jag **vill** komma. | I want to come. |

Compare:

Jag vill att du kommer.                    I want you to come.

**Att** may, but need not, be placed after the verbs **börja** 'begin' and **sluta** 'stop'.

| | |
|---|---|
| Vi **börjar** (att) arbeta kl. 8. | We start work at 8. |
| Det **började** (att) regna, när vi gick hemifrån. | It started to rain when we left home. |
| Vi **slutar** (att) arbeta kl. 5. | We stop work at 5. |
| Det **slutade** (att) regna, när vi kom fram. | It stopped raining when we arrived. |

The infinitive is also used in the following three constructions, where English uses the 'ing' form after a preposition, or the infinitive:

**genom att** 'by'

| | |
|---|---|
| Vi väckte Tina **genom att ropa** hennes namn. | We woke Tina up by shouting her name. |

**utan att** 'without'

| | |
|---|---|
| Lisa gick **utan att säga** adjö. | Lisa went without saying goodbye. |
| Peter tjänade mycket pengar **utan att** egentligen **anstränga sig.** | Peter made a lot of money without really exerting himself. |

**för att** '(in order) to'

| | |
|---|---|
| Lilla Per måste ställa sig på en stol **för att nå** kakburken. | Little Per had to stand on a chair to reach the cake tin. |
| **För att vinna** måste ni träna hårdare. | (In order) to win you will have to train harder. |

## 16.2 *Att* clauses and the infinitive as subject

When an **att** clause or an infinitive acts as subject there are two alternative constructions in Swedish:

| | |
|---|---|
| **Att Eva vann tävlingen,** förvånade alla. | (The fact) that Eva won the competition surprised everyone. |
| **Det** förvånade alla, **att Eva vann tävlingen.** | It surprised everyone that Eva won the competition. |
| **Att simma** är roligt. | Swimming is fun. |
| **Det** är roligt **att simma.** | It is fun to swim. |

An **att** clause or infinitive construction is often placed at the end of the sentence, and the normal subject position is filled by **det**. Because this is not the real subject, it is termed the *'formal subject'* *(formellt subjekt)* (see 3.3). Here are some more examples:

| | |
|---|---|
| **Att Per inte hade ringt,** irriterade Maria. | That Per had not rung irritated Maria. |
| **Det** irriterade Maria, **att Per inte hade ringt.** | It irritated Maria that Per had not rung. |
| **Att vänta på någon** är tråkigt. | Waiting for someone is boring. |
| **Det** är tråkigt **att vänta på någon.** | It is boring to wait for someone. |

The construction with the formal subject **det** is, in fact, the more common. If you want to make a yes/no question this alternative is the only possible one:

| | |
|---|---|
| Är **det** roligt **att simma?** | Is it fun to swim? |

As these constructions are fairly complicated, it pays to learn the commonest expressions of this type as a kind of fixed structure into which you can fit an **att** clause or an infinitive. (In the following list the past form of the verb is given in brackets.)

**1.** Expressions followed by an **att** clause

**Det sägs (sades) att**

| | |
|---|---|
| Det sägs att hon är väldigt förmögen. | She is said to be very wealthy. |

**Det påstås (påstods) att**

| | |
|---|---|
| Det påstods att regeringen tänkte avgå. | It was claimed that the government was going to resign. |

**Det syns (syntes) att**

| | |
|---|---|
| Det syns att Karin är trött. | You can see that Karin is tired. |

**Det hörs (hördes) att**

| | |
|---|---|
| Det hördes att Per var ledsen. | You could hear that Per was upset. |

Note, too, the following expressions of *probability:*

| | | |
|---|---|---|
| | osannolikt<br>unlikely | |
| | möjligt<br>possible | |
| Det är<br>It is | sannolikt<br>probable, likely | att X-partiet vinner valet.<br>that the X party will win the election. |
| | troligt<br>likely | |
| | säkert<br>certain | |

This construction is an alternative to using an adverbial (see 6.7), as in the following examples:

| X-partiet vinner<br>The X party will | knappast<br>hardly<br>möjligen<br>possibly<br>kanske<br>perhaps<br>sannolikt<br>probably<br>troligen<br>probably<br>säkert<br>certainly | valet.<br>win the election. |
|---|---|---|

**2. Expressions followed by an att clause or an infinitive**

These constructions often express an *attitude* or *judgement* (what you think about something).

**Det är (var) roligt att** 'It is nice that', 'It is fun to'

Det var roligt att du kunde komma.  It is nice that you could come.
Det är roligt att meta.  It is fun to fish.

**Det är (var) tråkigt att** 'It is a pity that', 'I am sorry that', 'It is annoying to'

Det är tråkigt att Maria är sjuk.  It is a pity that Maria is ill.
Det är alltid tråkigt att förlora.  It is always annoying to lose.

**Det är (var) kul att** (informal) 'It is nice that', 'It is fun to'

Det var kul att alla tyckte om  It was nice that everybody liked
maten.  the food.
Det är kul att åka skidor.  It is fun to go skiing.

**Det är (var) synd att** 'It is a pity that', It is a shame to'

Det är synd att vi redan måste  It is a pity we have to go home
åka hem.  already.
Det är synd att behöva avliva  It is a shame to have to put away
en hund, som har blivit gammal.  a dog that has grown old.

**Det är (var) bra att** 'It is a good thing that', 'It is a good idea to'

Det var bra att du kom ihåg hans  It is a good thing you remembered
födelsedag.  his birthday.
Det är alltid bra att ha ett  It is always a good idea to have
reservdäck i bilen.  a spare tyre in the car.

Note that Swedish often uses the past tense in expressions of this kind in a rather unexpected way. The past expresses a subjective reaction, what you think about something you have just found out about:

| | |
|---|---|
| – Jag kan tyvärr inte komma på festen imorgon. | I'm afraid I can't come to the party tomorrow. |
| – Det **var** tråkigt. | That's a pity. |

| | |
|---|---|
| – Jan har vunnit på tipset. | Jan has won the pools. |
| – Det **var** roligt att höra. | That's nice. |

When you welcome a guest at the door, you can say:

| | |
|---|---|
| Det **var** roligt att du kunde komma. | How nice that you could come. |

If you unexpectedly meet an old friend in the street who you haven't seen for some time, you can say (informally):

| | |
|---|---|
| Det **var** kul att se dig igen. | Nice to see you again. |

**3.** Expressions followed only by an infinitive

**Det är (var) svårt att** 'It is difficult to'

| | |
|---|---|
| Det var svårt att sluta röka. | It was difficult to stop smoking. |

**Det är (var) lätt att** 'It is easy to'

| | |
|---|---|
| Det är lätt att lära sig dansa. | It is easy to learn to dance. |

**Det går (gick) att** 'It is possible to'

| | |
|---|---|
| Det går inte att öppna det här fönstret. | It is not possible to open this window. |

## 16.3 Important verbs followed by an *att* clause or the infinitive as object

**Att** clauses as object have already been described in 7.3.

**1.** a) **tycka, tro** and **tänka**

The verbs **tycka, tro** and **tänka** are discussed here because it is difficult for students to distinguish between them.

**Tycka** is used when the sub-clause expresses an attitude or judgement on the part of the person who is the subject of the verb. The nearest equivalent in English is 'think', 'be of the opinion':

| | |
|---|---|
| Jag tyckte att filmen var bra. | I thought the film was good. |
| Jag tycker att Maria borde gå hem. | I think Maria ought to go home. |

**Tro,** which corresponds to 'think' in the sense of 'believe', 'imagine', is used when the idea expressed in the sub-clause is about a point of fact:

| | |
|---|---|
| Jag trodde att filmen var regisserad av Ingmar Bergman | I thought the film was directed by Ingmar Bergman. |
| Jag tror att Maria vill gå hem nu. | I think Maria wants to go home now. |

**Tycka** is not possible in the last two sentences, as there is no judgement involved.

The English verb 'think' corresponds to the Swedish verb **tänka** when a mental process is involved:

| | |
|---|---|
| Hon tänker alltid på sina barn. | She always thinks of her children. |
| Vi tänker resa hem ikväll. | We are thinking of going home this evening. |
| Stör mig inte! Jag tänker. | Don't disturb me. I'm thinking. |

Compare also:

| | |
|---|---|
| Jag tänker på dig. | I'm thinking of you. |
| Jag tror på dig. | I believe you. |
| Har han kommit? – Jag tror det. | Has he come? – I think so. |
| Är det vackert? – Jag tycker det. | Is it beautiful? – I think so. |

### b) veta, kunna and känna

The verb 'know' in general corresponds to the Swedish verb **veta** when used before a subordinate clause:

| | |
|---|---|
| Eva vet att du är galen i Mozart. | Eva knows that you are crazy about Mozart. |

There are, however, several important constructions where it has other equivalents:

| | |
|---|---|
| Eva kan engelska. (See 6.3.) | Eva knows (speaks) English. |
| Jag kan simma, men jag kan inte just nu. | I can (know how to) swim, but I can't right now. |
| Lisa känner Jan. | Lisa knows Jan. |

Compare:

| | |
|---|---|
| Lisa kände att hon var trött. | Lisa felt that she was tired. |

### 2. Verbs denoting promising, commanding and advising

After the verb **lova** 'promise' two constructions are possible:

| | |
|---|---|
| Jag lovar att komma i tid. | I promise to come in time. |
| Jag lovar att jag ska komma i tid. | I promise that I'll come in time. |

The first construction uses **att** + the infinitive. Note that, as usual, the infinitive has no subject. The other possibility is to use an **att** clause, as in the second example. In this case there must be a subject in the subordinate clause.

In addition, in subordinate clauses after **lova** and other similar verbs a form of the auxiliary verb **ska** 'shall', 'will' (**skulle** 'should', 'would') is used. If the verb in the main clause is in the present, the present form **ska** is used; if the verb in the main clause is in the past, the past form **skulle** is used, as in the following example:

| | |
|---|---|
| Jag lovade att jag **skulle** komma i tid. | I promised that I would come in time. |

Alternatively you can use the infinitive:

| | |
|---|---|
| Jag lovade att komma i tid. | I promised to come in time. |

Note that it is also possible in Swedish to put a person object after **lova**, followed by the infinitive construction. This is not possible in English:

| | |
|---|---|
| Jag lovade honom att komma i tid. | I promised him that I would come in time. |

Other verbs which have the same constructions as **lova** are those that denote a command or advice:

**be** 'ask'

| | |
|---|---|
| Jag bad henne att öppna fönstret. Jag bad henne att hon skulle öppna fönstret. | I asked her to open the window. |

**säga åt** 'tell'

| | |
|---|---|
| Du måste säga åt dem att vara försiktiga. Du måste säga åt dem att de ska vara försiktiga. | You must tell them to be careful. |

**beordra, befalla** 'order'

| | |
|---|---|
| Kaptenen beordrade oss att springa runt kasernen. | The captain ordered us to run round the barrack block. |

**råda** 'advise'

| | |
|---|---|
| Vi rådde Per att sälja villan. Vi rådde Per att han skulle sälja villan. | We advised Per to sell the house. |

Since the infinitive construction is the easier one, it is probably a good idea to learn it first when you make sentences of your own. But you will have to be able to understand the other construction, as that, too, is fairly common.

### 3. se, höra and känna

After the verbs **se** 'see', **höra** 'hear', and **känna** 'feel', the **att** construction and, after an object, the infinitive construction are used:

| | |
|---|---|
| Jag såg att han kom. | I saw him come (coming). |
| Jag såg honom komma. | I saw him come (coming). |
| Jag såg att Eva tvättade bilen. | I saw that Eva was washing her car. |
| Jag såg Eva tvätta bilen. | I saw Eva wash (washing) her car. |
| Eva hörde att Per sjöng nubbevisor. | Eva heard that Per was singing drinking songs. |
| Eva hörde Per sjunga nubbevisor. | Eva heard Per sing (singing) drinking songs. |

| Jag känner att en myra kryper uppför mitt ben. | I can feel that an ant is crawling up my leg. |
|---|---|
| Jag känner en myra krypa uppför mitt ben. | I can feel an ant crawling up my leg. |

Note that there is no **att** before the infinitive when the infinitive follows the verbs **se, höra** and **känna.**

**4.** Verbs denoting trying, succeeding, failing and the like

The following verbs are also constructed with an infinitive expression as the object. After some of these verbs the **att** is optional.

**försöka** 'try'

| Anna försökte (att) laga lampan. | Anna tried to mend the lamp. |
|---|---|

**lyckas** 'succeed', 'manage'

| Fred lyckades (att) öppna locket. | Fred succeeded in opening (managed to open) the lid. |
|---|---|

**misslyckas med** 'fail'

| Vi misslyckades med att sälja bilen. | We failed to sell the car. |
|---|---|

**hinna** 'manage', 'have time'

| Ingen hann (att) se vad han gjorde. | No one managed to see what he did. |
|---|---|

**våga** 'dare'

| Vem vågar (att) hoppa först? | Who dares to jump first? |
|---|---|

**undvika** 'avoid'

| Han undviker alltid att tala om obehagliga saker. | He always avoids talking about unpleasant things. |
|---|---|

**undgå** 'escape'

| Vi undgick precis att bli överkörda av tåget. | We just escaped being run over by the train. |
|---|---|

**tvinga** 'force'

| Polisen tvingade honom att erkänna. | The police forced him to confess. |
|---|---|

**förmå** 'persuade'

| Vem kan förmå Peter att komma hit? | Who can persuade Peter to come here? |
|---|---|

**vägra** 'refuse'

| Den misstänkte vägrade att svara på några frågor. | The suspect refused to answer any questions. |
|---|---|

## 16.4 Indirect questions

The questions which have already been discussed (4.2–4.3) are *direct questions (direkta frågor)*. By direct question we mean a real question that we expect an answer to. But there are also *indirect questions (indirekta frågor)*, which are a kind of report of direct questions. In fact, indirect questions are a kind of statement that does not expect an answer. Compare the following direct and indirect questions:

| *Direct question* | *Indirect question* |
|---|---|
| Vem träffade hon igår? | Jag undrar vem hon träffade igår. |
| Who did she meet yesterday? | I wonder who she met yesterday. |
| Vad gör du? | Jag kan se vad du gör. |
| What are you doing? | I can see what you are doing. |
| Är Ulla hemma? | Per vet om Ulla är hemma. |
| Is Ulla at home? | Per knows if Ulla is at home. |

Indirect questions are subordinate clauses which follow the word order of subordinate clauses, that is, the subject must always come before the verb. Thus they differ from direct questions, which are always main clauses and which have a special word order – verb before subject. Usually an indirect question functions as the object of a verb like **undra** 'wonder', **fråga** 'ask', **veta** 'know', **se** 'see' and **höra** 'hear'. When we discussed direct questions, we made a distinction between yes/no questions and question-word questions. This distinction is also important when describing indirect questions.


## 16.5 Indirect yes/no questions

Indirect yes/no questions in Swedish have a completely different form from direct yes/no questions. They are introduced by a special conjunction, **om** 'if', 'whether'. This is the same word as is used in another type of subordinate clause, the conditional clause (see 7.4). Compare the following examples:

| *Direct question* | *Indirect question* |
|---|---|
| Kommer du hit imorgon? | Per undrar om du kommer hit imorgon. |
| Are you coming here tomorrow? | Per wonders if you are coming here tomorrow. |
| Har någon sett Kerstin? | Vi vill veta om någon har sett Kerstin. |
| Has anyone seen Kerstin? | We want to know if anyone has seen Kerstin. |
| Regnar det? | Jag vet inte om det regnar. |
| Is it raining? | I don't know if it is raining. |

The rule is:

---

An indirect yes/no question is introduced by **om** and always has the subject before the verb.

---

## 16.6 Indirect question-word questions

An indirect question-word question is introduced by a question word (q-word), but here the subject always comes before the verb. This means that you can tell a direct from an indirect question-word question by the word order. As you know, in a direct question the subject must come after the verb.

| *Direct q-word question* | *Indirect q-word question* |
|---|---|
| När kom Peter hem? | När Peter kom hem, vet jag inte. |
| When did Peter come home? | I don't know when Peter came home. |
| Vad hade han gjort? | Vad han hade gjort, vet jag inte. |
| What had he done? | I don't know what he had done. |

There is a complication when the question word functions as the subject in the indirect question. In this case a word is put in after the question word; this is the word **som** – the same word that is used to introduce a relative clause. Compare the following examples:

| *Direct q-word question* | *Indirect q-word question* |
|---|---|
| Vem kom? | Jag såg, vem **som** kom. |
| Who came? | I saw who came. |
| Vad har hänt? | Vi vill veta, vad **som** har hänt. |
| What has happened? | We want to know what has happened. |
| Vems väska står där? | Per undrar, vems väska **som** |
| Whose case is that? | står där. |
| | Per wonders whose case that is. |

In the last example the question word is part of the subject. In this case the **som** in the indirect question is placed immediately after the last word in the subject.

The **som** which is put in after the subject makes a clear distinction between a direct and an indirect question when the word order alone does not signal the difference.

| Vem kom? | Who came? |
|---|---|
| Vem som kom, vet jag inte | I don't know who came. |

The rule is:

---

In indirect questions the word **som** is inserted after the subject when the question word is the subject or part of the subject.

---

The following diagram shows what is special about word order in indirect question-word questions:

| Q-WORD | SUBJECT | VERB |
|---|---|---|
| Jag undrar, vem | hon | ska träffa. |
| I wonder who she is going to meet. | | |
| Jag undrar, vem | **som** | ska träffa henne. |
| I wonder who is going to meet her. | | |
| Jag undrar, vad | du | gör. |
| I wonder what you are doing. | | |
| Jag undrar, vad | **som** | finns i den här lådan. |
| I wonder what there is in this drawer. | | |
| Jag undrar, vilken väg | du | brukar ta. |
| I wonder which way you usually go. | | |
| Jag undrar vilket program | **som** | kommer sedan. |
| I wonder what program comes next. | | |

When the question word is the subject or part of the subject, we can imagine that the subject as a whole moves up to the question-word position first in the subordinate clause. The subject position is then empty, but as a Swedish clause must have a subject, this place is filled by **som**. **Som** can therefore be looked upon as a replacement for the subject (compare 3.3).

# 16.7 Relative clauses

Relative clauses were first presented briefly in 7.6. Usually relative clauses are introduced by the word **som**, 'who', 'which', 'that' which never changes its form:

| | |
|---|---|
| Eva tyckte inte om filmen **som** visades på TV. | Eva did not like the film that (which) was shown on TV. |
| Jag vill ha tillbaka boken **som** du lånade i förra veckan. | I'd like the book back that you borrowed last week. |
| Middagen **som** vi åt på hotellet var fantastisk. | The dinner we had at the hotel was fantastic. |
| Barnen **som** lekte på gården har gjort en snögubbe. | The children who were playing in the yard have made a snowman. |
| Ministern **som** hade framlagt förslaget angreps häftigt av oppositionen. | The minister who had made the proposal was violently attacked by the opposition. |

The word **som** is omitted fairly often in relative clauses, just as 'who', 'that' and 'which' can be left out in English in certain clauses. The rule is that whenever you can leave out the relative in English, you can also leave out **som** in Swedish.

Mannen ni söker är inte här.    =    Mannen som ni söker är inte här.
The man you are looking for is not here.    The man that you are looking for is not here.

| Väskan jag köpte igår är för liten. = | Väskan som jag köpte igår är för liten. |
|---|---|
| The bag I bought yesterday is too small. | The bag that I bought yesterday is too small. |
| Mannen polisen grep igår har ännu inte erkänt. = | Mannen som polisen grep igår har ännu inte erkänt. |
| The man the police arrested yesterday has not yet confessed. | The man who the police arrested yesterday has not yet confessed. |

**Som** cannot always be left out. The most important condition for omission is that there must be a subject after **som** in the relative clause. If there is no subject, as in the following example, **som** cannot be left out:

| Jag känner igen mannen **som** står därborta. | I recognize the man who is standing over there. |
|---|---|

To denote place **där** can be used as a relative (compare 15.1). With this function it corresponds to 'where' or 'in which' in English. Note that the question word **var** described in 4.4 can never be used as a relative in Swedish:

| Huset **där** de bor ska rivas. | The house where they live is to be pulled down. |
|---|---|
| Den lilla staden **där** jag föddes heter Trosa. | The little town where I was born is called Trosa. |

For a point in time, **när** or **då** 'when' are used as relatives:

| Den här morgonen **när** (**då**) vi kom till den lilla byn, sov alla ännu. | The morning (when) we came to the little village everyone was still asleep. |
|---|---|

The word **vilken** (**vilket, vilka**), which was described in 13.2, can also be used as a relative, but it often sounds rather formal and is mainly found in the written language. Normally **som** can be used instead, so just learn to understand relative clauses introduced by **vilken**, but avoid using them:

| Mannen, **vilken** länge hade varit deprimerad, försvann från sitt hem i onsdags. | The man, who had been depressed for a long time, disappeared from his home last Wednesday. |
|---|---|
| Förslaget, **vilket** tidigare hade väckt en hård debatt, antogs till slut. | The proposal, which had previously led to a stormy debate, was finally accepted. |
| Medlemmarna, **vilka** tidigare hade varit emot förslaget, hade insett dess fördelar. | The members, who had previously been against the proposal, had realized its advantages. |

145

## 16.8 Isolated prepositions

When you place a phrase which begins with a preposition at the beginning of a sentence (4.6) the preposition can sometimes be left on its own in the place where the phrase usually comes in the sentence:

Jag tänker alltid **på dig.**
**På dig** tänker jag alltid.       I'm always thinking of you.
**Dig** tänker jag alltid **på.**

Man kan öppna alla dörrar **med**
**den här nyckeln.**
**Med den här nyckeln** kan man    You can open all doors with
öppna alla dörrar.                 this key.
**Den här nyckeln** kan man öppna
alla dörrar **med.**

Practise understanding sentences like these, as they are fairly common. However, it is not always possible to leave the preposition on its own, so wait until you are quite sure when it is possible before you try yourself.

When the phrase which is being asked about contains a preposition, this preposition is normally left in the place it has in an ordinary statement. As you can see, the same is true in English:

Alla verkar vänta **på någon. Vem**    Everybody seems to be waiting
väntar de **på**?                      for someone. Who are they
                                       waiting for?

**Vem** bodde du **hos** i Malmö?       Who did you stay with in Malmö?
– Jag bodde **hos min syster.**         – I stayed with my sister.
**Vem** pratar du **med**?              Who are you talking to?
– Jag pratar **med Maria.**             – I'm talking to Maria.

As in more formal English, the preposition can also come before the question word, as in the example below. But this is rather unusual in Swedish. For question-word questions the main rule is: leave the preposition in its normal place in the sentence.

**Med vem** pratade du?         To whom did you speak?
(Possible but should be avoided)

The preposition also stands on its own in indirect question-word questions (see 16.6):

Eva frågade **vem** jag pratade **med.**    Eva asked who I talked to.
Jag undrar **vad** han tänker **på.**       I wonder what he's thinking about.

A preposition can never come before **som** in a relative clause. It must stand on its own in its normal place in the sentence. This rule also applies when the **som** is omitted:

| | |
|---|---|
| Flickan som jag pratade **med** heter Maria. | The girl that I was talking to is called Maria. |
| Alternatively: | |
| Flickan jag pratade **med** heter Maria. | The girl I was talking to is called Maria. |
| Våningen (som) vi tittade **på** igår verkade trevlig. | The flat we looked at yesterday seemed nice. |
| Mannen (som) alla väntade **på** utanför biografen var huvud-rollsinnehavaren. | The man everybody was waiting for outside the cinema was the star. |

**Som** + preposition on its own can often be used as an alternative to **där** when you refer to a place:

| | |
|---|---|
| Huset **som** de bor **i** ska rivas. | The house they live in is to be pulled down. |
| Huset **där** de bor ska rivas. | The house where they live is to be pulled down. |

147

# 17 Cleft and existential sentences

## 17.1 The cleft sentence

If you want to emphasize a particular part of a clause, you can use the *cleft sentence,* so called because it splits a clause into two parts, each with its own verb.

| | |
|---|---|
| Det är Maria som har målat tavlan. | It is Maria that (who) painted the picture. |
| Det var den här skjortan som jag köpte i morse. | It was this shirt (that) I bought this morning. |

The cleft sentence construction usually begins with **det är** (or **det var**, if in the past) followed by the word or phrase which you want to emphasize.

**Det** $\begin{Bmatrix} \text{är} \\ \text{var} \end{Bmatrix}$ _____ **som** _____
(rest of sentence)

| | |
|---|---|
| Peter såg en älg igår. | Peter saw a moose yesterday. |
| Det var **Peter** som såg en älg igår. | It was Peter that saw a moose yesterday. |
| Det var **en älg** som Peter såg igår. | It was a moose that Peter saw yesterday. |
| | |
| Eva bor här. | Eva lives here. |
| Det är **Eva** som bor här. | It is Eva that lives here. |
| Det är **här** som Eva bor. | It is here that Eva lives. |

The same rules as in a relative clause apply concerning the omission of **som**: **som** can be omitted if it is followed by a subject:

| | |
|---|---|
| Det är här Eva bor. | It is here Eva lives. |
| Det var igår Peter såg en älg. | It was yesterday Peter saw a moose. |

If the phrase which is emphasized contains a preposition, you can often choose between moving the whole expression forward or leaving the preposition behind:

| | |
|---|---|
| Jag talade **med Maria.** | I spoke to Maria. |
| Det var **med Maria** (som) jag talade. | It was to Maria I spoke. |
| Det var **Maria** (som) jag talade **med.** | It was Maria (that) I spoke to. |

Only **som** can be used in this construction, not **där, då, när** or **vilken** (compare 16.7).

| | |
|---|---|
| Det är i det där huset (som) de bor. | It is in that house they live. |
| Det är det där huset (som) de bor i. | It is that house they live in. |
| Det var i tisdags (som) Jan kom. | It was last Tuesday (that) Jan came. |

The cleft sentence structure can be used in yes/no questions:

| | |
|---|---|
| Är det Maria som har målat tavlan? | Is it Maria that has painted the picture? |
| Var det igår (som) Peter såg en älg? | Was it yesterday (that) Peter saw a moose? |

It is also fairly common in Swedish to use the cleft sentence structure in question-word questions.

| *Q-word question* | *Cleft sentence* |
|---|---|
| Vem kommer?<br>Who is coming? | Vem är det som kommer?<br>Who is it that is coming? |
| Vem såg dig?<br>Who saw you? | Vem var det som såg dig?<br>Who was it that saw you? |
| Vem såg du?<br>Who did you see? | Vem var det som du såg?<br>Who was it (that) you saw? |

The cleft sentence structure is particularly used in those questions where it might otherwise be difficult to know which was the subject and which was the object. In the following question-word question **vem** can be interpreted as either the subject or the object:

Vem såg Eva?
*could mean either*

| | |
|---|---|
| Vem var det som såg Eva? | Who was it that saw Eva? |

*or*

| | |
|---|---|
| Vem var det som Eva såg? | Who was it (that) Eva saw? |

Even though English has a similar construction, the cleft sentence in Swedish may seem a little tricky at first. But it is very important that you learn at least to understand sentences that use this construction, as it is very common.

## 17.2 The existential sentence

In Swedish, as in English, a special construction is used when you want to introduce new persons or things into the conversation. This construction is the *existential sentence (presentering* or *existentialsats)*. Instead of beginning the sentence with the real subject, you begin it with a formal subject, the word **det** 'there'. Then follow the verb and the real subject:

(**En bil** kommer på vägen.)
(A car is coming along the road.)

**Det** kommer **en bil** på vägen.
There is a car coming along the road.

(**Någon** är i trädgården)
(Someone is in the garden.)

**Det** är **någon** i trädgården.
There is someone in the garden.

The sentences in brackets on the left are not wrong in Swedish or English, but in both languages the existential sentences on the right are considered better.

Thus the usual equivalent of English **there is** and **there are** is the Swedish **det är.** However, as can be seen from the first example above, other verbs than **är** can accompany **det** in this construction. The verb **finnas (finns, fanns, funnits)** is perhaps the commonest. This verb says that something exists, but it usually corresponds to the verb 'be' in English:

| | |
|---|---|
| **Det finns** öl i kylen. | There is beer in the fridge. |
| **Det finns** över 8 miljoner människor i Sverige. | There are over 8 million people in Sweden. |
| **Det fanns** ett torp här för länge sedan. | There was a cottage here a long time ago. |
| **Det har** aldrig **funnits** vilda lejon i Sverige. | There have never been wild lions in Sweden. |

The existential sentence structure can be used to form a question if the word **det** is placed after the verb:

| | |
|---|---|
| Är det någon i trädgården? | Is there anyone in the garden? |
| Finns det öl i kylen? | Is there any beer in the fridge? |

Existential sentences often contain verbs with the following meanings:

*Existence:* **finnas** (and its opposites **saknas** and **fattas** 'be lacking', 'be missing')
*Position:* **vara** 'be', **bo** 'live', **sitta** 'sit', **stå** 'stand', **ligga** 'lie', **hänga** 'hang'
*Movement:* **komma** 'come', **gå** 'go', **simma** 'swim'

| | |
|---|---|
| **Det finns** potatis i köket. | There are potatoes in the kitchen. |
| **Det saknas** en knapp i rocken. | There is a button missing from the coat. |
| **Det är** mycket folk här idag. | There are a lot of people here today. |
| **Bor det** någon i det gamla torpet? | Is there anyone living in the old cottage? |

| | |
|---|---|
| **Det sitter** en katt i trappan. | There is a cat sitting on the steps. |
| **Kommer det** ofta lapplisor på den här gatan? | Do traffic wardens often come down this street? |
| **Det hänger** en tavla på väggen. | There is a picture hanging on the wall. |
| **Det går** ett tåg i timmen till Malmö. | A train goes every hour to Malmö. (There is a train every hour to Malmö.) |
| **Det simmar** en and i dammen. | There is a duck swimming in the pond. |

As you can see from the above examples, Swedish uses the existential sentence structure with certain verbs where English prefers to use the 'there is' construction or a straightforward subject-verb construction.

Note that the verbs **ligga, stå** and **sitta** can be used about things in Swedish (see 15.2):

| | |
|---|---|
| **Det ligger** en tidning på golvet. | There is a newspaper (lying) on the floor. |
| **Det står** en lampa i hörnet. | There is a lamp in the corner. |
| **Det sitter** några blanketter i pärmen. | There are some forms in the file. |
| **Ligger det** några pengar på bordet? | Is there any money on the table? |

## 17.3 When can you use the existential sentence?

There are certain conditions for using the existential sentence structure:

**1. The subject must be new.**

The existential sentence structure is used by a speaker for the purpose of drawing the listener's attention to some person or thing that is new or unknown to him. This fact is normally indicated by the real subject having the indefinite article or no article at all if it is an uncountable noun or a noun in the plural.

| | |
|---|---|
| (**En flicka** sitter på bänken.) (A girl is sitting on the bench.) | Det sitter **en flicka** på bänken. There is a girl sitting on the bench. |
| (**Några flickor** bor i lägenheten.) (Some girls live in the flat.) | Det bor **några flickor** i lägenheten. There are some girls living in the flat. |
| (**Kött** finns i frysen.) (Meat is in the fridge.) | Det finns **kött** i frysen. There is meat in the fridge. |

Just as in English, the real subject cannot be an NP in the definite form, nor proper names, personal pronouns or nouns with a possessive pronoun or the genitive, since such nouns represent known things.

151

*Known subject*

**Flickan**
**Eva**
**Hon** } sitter på bänken.          *Wrong:* Det sitter flickan . . .
**Kalles flicka**
**Hans flicka**

**Köttet** finns i frysen.          *Wrong:* Det finns köttet . . .

---

Existential sentences must have an indefinite NP as subject.

---

2. The verb must not have an object.

En flicka öppnar fönstret.          *Wrong:* Det öppnar . . .
A girl opens the window.

Några flickor läser tidningen.          *Wrong:* Det läser . . .
Some girls are reading the paper.

En katt slickar sin päls.          *Wrong:* Det slickar . . .
A cat is licking its coat.

# Index

The figures refer to page numbers.
Figures in italics indicate the pages where
the points are dealt with in greater detail.

*Appendices*

# THE SWEDISH ALPHABET

| Uppercase Letters | Lowercase Letters | Letter Names |
|:---:|:---:|:---:|
| A | a | a |
| B | b | be |
| C | c | se |
| D | d | de |
| E | e | e |
| F | f | eff |
| G | g | ge |
| H | h | hå |
| I | i | i |
| J | j | ji |
| K | k | kå |
| L | l | ell |
| M | m | em |
| N | n | en |
| O | o | o |
| P | p | pe |
| Q | q | ku |
| R | r | ärr |
| S | s | ess |
| T | t | te |
| U | u | u |
| V | v | ve |
| X | x | eks |
| Y | y | y |
| Z | z | säta |
| Å | å | å |
| Ä | ä | ä |
| Ö | ö | ö |

Vowels

Consonants

# NUMBERS

Cardinal Numbers

| | |
|---|---|
| 1 = ett, en |
| 2 = två |
| 3 = tre |
| 4 = fyra |
| 5 = fem |
| 6 = sex |
| 7 = sju |
| 8 = åtta |
| 9 = nio |
| 10 = tio |
| 11 = elva |
| 12 = tolv |
| 13 = tretton |
| 14 = fjorton |
| 15 = femton |
| 16 = sexton |
| 17 = sjutton |
| 18 = arton |
| 19 = nitton |
| 20 = tjugo |
| 21 = tjugoett, tjugoen |
| 22 = tjugotvå |
| 23 = tjugotre |
| 24 = tjugofyra |
| 25 = tjugofem |
| 26 = tjugosex |
| 27 = tjugosju |
| 28 = tjugoåtta |
| 29 = tjugonio |
| 30 = trettio, tretti |
| 31 = trettiett, trettien |
| 40 = fyrtio, fyrti |
| 50 = femtio, femti |
| 60 = sextio, sexti |
| 70 = sjuttio, sjutti |
| 80 = åttio, åtti |
| 90 = nittio, nitti |
| 100 = (ett) hundra |
| 200 = två hundra |
| 250 = tvåhundrafemti |
| 1 000 = (ett) tusen |
| 10 000 = tio tusen |
| 100 000 = (ett) hundra tusen |

Ordinal Numbers

| | |
|---|---|
| 1 första |
| 2 andra |
| 3 tredje |
| 4 fjärde |
| 5 femte |
| 6 sjätte |
| 7 sjunde |
| 8 åttonde |
| 9 nionde |
| 10 tionde |
| 11 elfte |
| 12 tolfte |
| 13 trettonde |
| 14 fjortonde |
| 15 femtonde |
| 16 sextonde |
| 17 sjuttonde |
| 18 artonde |
| 19 nittonde |
| 20 tjugonde |
| 21 tjugoförsta |
| 22 tjugoandra |
| 23 tjugotredje |
| 24 tjugofjärde |
| 25 tjugofemte |
| 26 tjugosjätte |
| 27 tjugosjunde |
| 28 tjugoåttonde |
| 29 tjugonionde |
| 30 trettionde |
| 31 trettiförsta |

$3658$ = tretusensexhundrafemtiåtta

159